"TRAINEE MILLIONAIRES WANTED"

(DIARY OF A NETWORK MARKETER)

PHILIPPA J.G. SYMES

Kate Bushell
2 Main Street
Shearsby
Lutterworth
Leics. LE17 6PJ
Tel: 0116 247 8160

Copyright © January 2000 by Philippa J.G. Symes

All rights reserved. No part of this publication may be reproduced, stored in a retrieval system, or transmitted in any form or by any means including photocopying, electronic, mechanical or otherwise without the written permission of the right holders, application for which must be made to the publisher.

Published by The Charlie Bear Publishing Company, Monmouth 2002

Printed in Great Britain by CPI

Acknowledgements

Some things are just meant to be. Some things just happen. The world keeps turning and another dawn will rise. This book has taken me two years to write, and I'd like to thank those people who have helped me both in my life and to contributing to this book.
My fabulous husband Robert who allows me the freedom to do what ever: a very special thank you. You have always stood by me and supported me in everything I have done. Thank you for having so much faith in me, I am so looking forward to all the years ahead of us and a wonderful future together. You will always be the person I turn to and I know you are always there for me. You have the patience of a saint and I love you dearly. Thank goodness one of us is logical! **Lawrence, Laura and my new daughter in-law Andrea**, I am blessed to have you all. My dream is that we shall all be living near each other (somewhere in the sun!) so that you can come and visit and I can hang out with you and take you shopping! Thank you for being just you.. I love you more than words can say! **My parents** for such immense kindness and always believing in me and for being there when I need you., rain or shine. You gave me the greatest gift of all: life. **Mel**, for being just you: simply the best. I wish you all the success you deserve, it's time for you to slow down and start enjoying life to the fullest, you are such a hard worker, and a wonderful person. **John and Jayne:** I am eternally grateful to have found two wonderful people who have shown me that life is truly for living to the full. There will never be enough thank you's for having so much belief in me and for all the help I need and continue to need. I strive to follow in your footsteps.. You are an inspiration and your knowledge in Network Marketing is truly phenomenal.I wish you both years of success, and hope in my heart that all your dreams come true, somehow I think they will!
Barry: Your words of encouragement have given me the determination to stick with this and see it through. Thanks for all your help in getting this to the finish line and I wish you all the very best life has to give!
And to all the special people in our team for all their hard work and effort, without whom *none* of this would be possible. You have been a pleasure to work with and I am so looking forward to seeing you all achieve your goals and dreams! Without you we simply wouldn't be where we are today. **Lizzie** – you are a true friend and will always be dear to me, thank you for always being there. **Jayne Thorburn** for being a dear buddy and for all the laughs we have had, I wish you the world.. What a trooper!

And finally, but not least to Bob Parker: An enormous thankyou for all your kind words and messages, and urging me to pursue this project, your enthusiasm gave me the courage to go ahead!

Diary of A Network Marketer

"Either you will be one of millions of ordinary men and women who achieve extraordinary lifestyles through Network Marketing or you'll be one of those who wish they had.."

Burke Hedges

INTRODUCTION

MONEY DOESN'T BUY HAPPINESS BUT IT SURE HELPS!

"So what is it that you do?" "Uh well, actually I'm a trainee millionaire".. You think I'm joking don't you? Ha! Well think again sunshine this is me, moi, millionaire in the making, and you know what? I'm having the time of my life! Whoever said money couldn't buy happiness doesn't know where to shop..

This is my first year in network marketing – wow, gosh, phew, man! what a year it has been! I cannot put into words just how much my life is changing, day by day, month by month but I'm going to try because it's just so amazing what can happen in a year. So here it is. Lock stock and all the smoking barrels.

It's important that you note that I am not as yet, some superstar having made it to the top of the marketing plan with profit share cheques coming out of my ears and all the bells and whistles. I have achieved a level of success for what that means to *me*, however, I recognise that I have a long journey ahead. Along the way, I've managed to build a team, and I've seen people discover things about themselves they didn't think they could do. I've made it to Manager on the compensation plan and I'm proud of that.. I go from strength to strength every day and I am a step closer to my dreams. So if you are reading this expecting triumph and glory at the end, this is not what this is about. It's about *my* journey, my first twelve months in network marketing and what it has meant to me. I've stuck to it, and I've survived. Everything else is just a matter of time…

Diary of A Network Marketer

Why did I write about this first year? Two reasons. Firstly, I never intended to write this book – it just happened. Finally I had something I could write about with passion, something that really seemed to make sense. It's been a goal I've always had but never followed through. I have always had this burning desire to write. I spent various phases of my life searching for inspiration and usually giving up in despair; children's books, love stories, thrillers, nothing really seemed to flow. Network Marketing together with FLP has opened up a whole new exciting chapter in my life. Whether my book ever reached the stage of being put into print was entirely another matter, I just wanted to say "hey! I've done it!" Amazing what can happen when you put things into action and really believe that actually you can do it.. Secondly, I wanted to share that first year, with all its trials and tribulations, and to send a message to say have the courage to keep going even when things are looking tough, and have that determination and stickability, to see things through.

When I began this journey, this passage of time, when someone (my sponsors and now mentors, an inspiration to all seeking light at the end of the darkest tunnel) opened up this chapter in January 2000, I was in a total daze, I wanted to know so much. I was presented with the most amazing opportunity on how I could change my life (our lives) that I really didn't know where I was going, what I was doing or how the hell to get there. All I could see was a fantastic opportunity to finally be free of debt, and to live a lifestyle that most of us seek, and few of us find. This year has been such a turning point in my life that I have decided to share it with you. I have read many books on Network Marketing these past 12 months; so many books to read and yet where on earth should I begin? Here I was on the adventure of a lifetime but where do you start when it comes to reading material? There were copious books on "Your first year in MLM" (what's MLM?) but they had all been written by now seasoned network marketers some of whom I've later learnt haven't even put into practice what they preach. There was nothing for people like ME, the novice, the new entrepreneur, no step by step guide on what it's *really* like, no telling it how it really is on a month to month basis, the ups and downs, the highs and lows – the here and now. And so here I am faced with a clean page and a head simply brimming with stuff. Things I want to share and my mind spinning with words. To that end I have embarked on putting pen to paper or rather to sitting in front of a computer and getting it all down. To maybe share a little on this past year's experiences, to one person's year: mine, as it unfolds like a flower in the spring.

Diary of A Network Marketer

What is it that *so* excites me about network marketing? I can see and understand now that it is a dynamic means of helping all of us get to where we wish to be in life – it is the most incredible vehicle in letting us dream again. Network Marketing I've discovered is about being in the right place at the right time, and timing is different for all of us. It's also about taking the opportunity at the right time too. When you present this unique business to the world, you are offering a gift, the gift of true freedom. If someone says no, maybe the time just isn't right – not now, anyway.

I know in my heart that five years from now, if not sooner, our lifestyle will have changed dramatically, giving us more time, freedom and choices than we have ever had. Time to enjoy life, time to enjoy each other and the freedom to travel. Suddenly the whole world seems to be a much, much brighter place. But the best thing of all is that network marketing allows us to help other people like us, achieve their goals no matter who or what they are.

And what of this year? My first year in Network Marketing with Forever Living has been truly incredible, a lifesaver, a journey, a way forward, an inspiration, and so very much more! It's been a meeting of the minds, and a moving of the soul - and so many fabulous people have crossed my path and become part of my life that if nothing else my life is richer. So here is a little book with snippets of info of how I struggled through this first year (happily, most of the time, I might add) without all the mind boggling schemes and terminology to get your head around. An honest and straightforward introduction to *my* first year in Network Marketing. We are each of us on a different journey and yours will be quite different from mine, but maybe the end goals are somewhat similar..

WHY ME, WHY NOW?

What made me take that step?
People get into Network Marketing for all sorts of different reasons, and mine is no different probably than to many of you. It all began in the cold light of day one January morning in 2000 - the dawn of the new millennium. I was sitting in my front room looking out at a cold grey sky and pondering the Universe. You know sometimes when you hit that all

time low and suddenly you wake up and realise you just aren't getting any younger and hey – life is whizzing by at top speed? Well all of that and more happened to me this year. Panic has set in. I've noticed I've got more grey hairs and I'm getting a bit forgetful, plus the added fact that now I really do have to hold paperwork at least a foot away to be able to read, (why are they typing in smaller font these days?) The years are simply gathering speed and I'm losing track of time..
I suddenly woke up - just like that. I was sort of in a time warp Dr. Who mode, and I looked back at the last 10 years and with horror couldn't really remember too much of what had gone on. I suppose it dawned on me in those few minutes, that life was far too short and one minute you are in your 30s and all of a sudden overnight you are 44. Well that's what happened to me anyway. I said to myself "Philippa, it's time to start living life, I mean *really* start living and stop procrastinating and putting everything off for a later day."

There I was in the January of a new year and looking at where we were heading and I came to the realisation that we were never going to actually reach any of our dreams if we continued on the path we were on; short of winning the lottery that is, or me becoming a famous rock star - (a lifelong ambition). How many times have I said *5 years from now I will be doing this that and the other* and guess what – here we are not *5 but 10 years later* and still no nearer to our hopes and dreams..OK so how many times have *you* said the same thing? I know I'm not alone here.

And so here we are, having lived the American Dream for 10 years on the East Coast of the Great US of A, and now back in the wet and grey of England with all its expense and high cost of living. Gone are the marghueritas by the pool and the hot humid days, of Charlie (our retriever) bobbing for pebbles in the pool and the kids getting dressed up for trick or treat and the sack loads of candies. Of Reeses Peanut butter and Philly cheesesteaks.. Gone are the continual blue skies and brilliant sunshine, the day trips to the bay to go sailing, and the all night shopping (not forgetting the sales and all the money I saved). Of watching fireflies at twilight, like fairy lights dancing all over the garden, and going to the canoe carnival on the lake in the heat and humidity in the darkest night, where lanterns flickered on the water from spectacular floats that balanced precariously on two canoes. A distant memory of crickets incessantly chirping in the midnight air, and the intensity of summer humidity. And winters of waking to deep deep snow and of trees and lakes of ice. Of

running around with the rescue squad as a volunteer Emergency Medical Technician in the middle of the night, sometimes up to three times a night, to cut people out of cars, knee deep in snow or in the freezing rain, to take overdose junkies to the hospital, to hold a frightened child - and maybe save a life.. Memories too sweet to savour at times. Ah, I can hear you say, but nothing compares to the beauty of the English countryside, and what about our Olde English pubs?
Well that's another story! So where am I? Oh yes, the here and now. Back in England and missing the good life....

JANUARY 2000
The beginning of the beginning

This year I am 44 – or am I 45?

Change is in the air, and I feel brighter already. The cold winter sun is still around, the air is refreshingly fresh, the sky is clear and blue and I just know that things are going to change. Don't ask me how, when or why, they just are.

I've made all my New Years Resolutions: lose 10 lbs, go easy on the alcohol, give up Cadburys cream eggs and all things chocolaty, taking time to put petrol in the car so I'm not running on fumes, oh and join a health club, and have Pamela Anderson's body.. I wonder how long I will last this year? This year I'm *determined* as always to make this year a year of change.

Reality check:
I suppose the majority of us all reach an all time low financially and emotionally some time in our lives, and for Robert and me it's now, January 2000. The business I eagerly started 18 months ago is struggling; actually that's the understatement of the year, it's crashing down around me and I still haven't broken even. The overdraft is mounting, and I'm running out of excuses with the bank manager (who incidentally has been incredibly considerate but then she's a woman so she has the connectivity thing). Horror of horrors I have to face up to the fact that I have to go back to work – full time, for *somebody else* no less. I can see this is going to be a challenge emotionally to say the least, the last thing on earth I want to do is get back into the rat race syndrome. It's not that long since I left it. I just hate getting up in the dark before I've finished sleeping, driving home in the dark and having to start all over again 12 hours later. It's ok when it's your own business it's quite another thing when you are doing it for someone else. Robert does it day in day out, and each day coming home with all that stress written all over his face and I can see it's really beginning to take its toll. There *has* to be a better way. There's just one problem: I really *don't* want to go back to work full time. I've had the luxury of working from home. What can I say, I've been spoilt. I have done many other things in life you know (exited the house). I've been a PA, a Business Development Exec, and been in Sales, Marketing, and

Diary of A Network Marketer

Advertising all my life before I set up my own business, plus I had the added glamour of working for a Radio Station and swanning around in a car with paw prints on (don't ask) Before I decided to take the plunge and start something on my own. So the last thing I need is the "Oh it's different for you" syndrome. Believe me I've done my hard graft in the real world.

So here we are back in the present and a dark cloud is looming on the horizon. Time waits for no man and it certainly isn't hanging around for me. It's come down to we either have to move, or I have to go back to work full time. Fact. Reality. Not enough money for the end of the month. Now I really don't want to take that route if I can possibly help it. I've just got to get out there and find that perfect job (I love being at home but I'll go stir crazy if I don't get the brain cells into gear), and bottom line: I want to stay at home and have a fantastic money making machine. Catch up on the ironing now and then (hate ironing but can't afford to farm it out), cook the occasional meal, and well you know, just generally be here for the kids even though they stay up in their rooms most of the time. Travel as and when, and have the best time ever. At the moment the days are packed with non-stop running around, and before you know it, it's 8 o'clock. Not only have I done the business, but I am Superwoman after all (yes they do exist), chief chef, taxi, cleaner, housekeeper, Psychologist, keeper of the peace, animal carer, sex goddess, friend, lover, brain surgeon, pooper scooper, politician, referee, agony aunt, trainee vet, nurse, the whole nine yards and *still* manage to run my own business.
And not a moment for moi.

So today, I've begun the beginning of weeks of trailing and ploughing through the newspapers just looking for something that stands out in a crowd. Usual stuff – boring, tedious jobs, but not for people like me. Hey! I want that impossible job; you know the one that pays you fantastic sums of money for doing very little, part time, naturally. I want a job where I can still work from home and potter around if I want to. Something that's fun, that I can do with other people, not just on my own. And by the way, I *am* prepared to work my wotsists off for the right thing. Does such a thing exist? Well it's a bit like the Holy Grail with me, I've been on this eternal mission to find the impossible, and I'm determined that I will eventually find it. It *has* to be out there somewhere. There's always stuffing envelopes after all. There has to be *something*. I briefly toyed a few months back with the idea of responding to a chain letter I received, you know the ones where you send off a pound and in five weeks you've made a million? I never took the chance, it just seemed a little too good to be true and there was always a nagging doubt at the back of my mind. I'm sure these things are illegal. And I'm so gullible.

Friday

There's an ad in the local paper today. You know the one that leaps out at you, the one you deliberately steer clear of because you know what it is. The one that says "WANTED" in large capitals and bold type. Inevitably get rich quick yeah, right. The ones you see littered around the small ads column in the Telegraph. The ones that scream out "hand over your money and your life!" However, I'm curious so I'm going to call, *now* in fact because I'm impatient and you just never know this *could* be it - the impossible dream! Which reminds me of a song I sung once in the States for my boss who was this mega CEO of the Number One Company in the top 100 of Americas greatest. He was short, bald and plump and loved deer hunting and making money, and later on I discovered went into speedboat racing God knows why, he didn't know how to race. He was an astute businessman though, he hung out with people who were successful and it seemed to have this rub on effect with him...

I digress..

I nonchalantly made the call, only to hear a taped message. But hang on, this is different, it isn't the usual hyped up salesman insisting that you drop everything and have got to hear this opportunity, to get rich in your first month! NO it's a gentle message, offering people a chance for change. I've left my name and number.

Saturday

I'm frustrated. Whoever it is with this wonderful opportunity hasn't bothered to call and now I'm starting to get anxious. I've called the number again and left another message. Oh well, I'm just going to get on with my life and keep looking.

Well eventually I did get a phone call almost a week later by which time I had decided that either they had been inundated by phone calls or I was at the bottom of the pile, or well maybe they just weren't interested. Good grief don't they know who I am? Reality is I can't understand why they aren't jumping at the bit to get me on board. I'm still highly sceptical, not going to be dragged into some con merchants idea of sucking me into some scheme where I have to part with tons of money. But I will confess I did have a pleasant conversation and on the surface it seems interesting and it could pave the way to a brighter and better future. It sounds good enough for me to at least meet up and find out more, in for a penny in for a pound and you never know this could be it, that once in a life time opportunity! (Ha!)

I'm meeting this chap next week, actually I'm quite excited now. I've got another five days to go.

January 15
What was five days seemed like an eternity because my interest had in fact been stirred. We met in a small café in town. I sat defensively across the coffee table, ready for the spiel. Arms folded with that knowing stare which smacked of "don't tell me how to suck eggs sunshine." With almost twenty-five years in sales and marketing I knew it all and I certainly had all the books and tapes, let alone the drawers full of t-shirts.

This very nice chap proceeded to present the business to me a non-persuasive direct and to the point way. It all sounded too good to be true and I was still extremely sceptical but something deep down was making my heart race – could this really be so good? It sounded so easy. Anyway dear heart, out came a tape and my heart sank. I'm really not into listening to somebody telling me the world is wonderful and this is the best opportunity ever. We engaged in a good five minutes of me pushing the tape back across the table saying sweetly that I didn't really want another tape – and John (that was his name) insisting that I really should listen to it. He won, (or rather I obliged), though I wasn't a pushover I can tell you.

Through three cups of coffee I proceeded to span out my brilliant record in sales only to be told categorically that if I was interested in this opportunity I had to take my salesman's hat off. *But I'm a pro* I insisted, I've made money, *tons* of money for companies, heck I used to sell fresh air, and brilliantly so! I'm *exactly* the person you need! John shook his head. He wasn't looking for salesmen, just ordinary people who were willing to learn. Different mindset. Mmm, interesting! This could be a challenge. I'm still highly sceptical but warming to the idea of change.

Then the bottom line:

Diary of A Network Marketer

"So what is it?" I asked
"Have you heard of Network Marketing?"
"Is it like Amway?" (My heart steadily sinking)
"No, Why do you ask?
"Well it just sounds familiar."
"Network Marketing is simply the marketing of products through a network of people, world-wide. It's lots and lots of people doing a little.."

I like that idea, it means I don't have to carry a garage full of stock and have to work like crazy to sell tons of products. I don't have to take on the world.

And I've discovered IT'S NOT PYRAMID SELLING!

Of course I haven't let on that I'm excited (that would be giving the game away,) but I am, incredibly so. I know in my heart that I've found something quite phenomenal. Well not *me* you understand but you get the picture. I've heard of Network Marketing before, but thought it was the dreaded pyramid selling, I'd also sort of had a go when I was living in the states with a cosmetic company, but had no support at all. It was like the blind leading the blind, so I had thrown in the towel. I've still got a box full of unused cosmetics that I've transported back over the Atlantic. So who is this company I have never heard of, this "Forever Living", and what do they do that's so special? Well, I have to say I'm really interested. Forever Living is (apparently) a company that "offers everyday consumable products in a fast growing market place" quote unquote.
A company that offers support and training, and most importantly a way to make a lot of money.
I'll repeat that.
And most importantly a way to make *a lot of money*. How *much* money exactly? No good beating about the bush because I need more than a few thousand pounds a month to get Rob out of his rotten job that's going to give him an early grave. It's not that I'm materialistic I hasten to add, but I don't want to work my socks off for five years and still be struggling. Being a cards on the table type of person, I asked this chap casually if he wouldn't mind sharing with me what he was earning. No point in wasting everyone's time! And let's face it, if the guy's been doing it a while he should be making the money by now. My time's precious you know.. Well I tried hard not to look too overwhelmed, I guess he's used to that question (perhaps not quite so blatant) and so he came prepared with

copies of recent cheques. I was impressed (it takes a lot to impress me), but I could live quite happily on fifteen thousand a month, (and that was just the tip of the iceberg)..

We parted company an hour later, me laden with information on the company the products and a promise of a phone call, and my mind in overdrive on what I could spend that amount of money on. I've already started thinking of having a second home somewhere idyllic with warm weather and blue skies year round. Spain maybe, or the South of France.. Still it could all be a big wind up and what was the bottom line anyway? I've toughened up over the years but I'm still gullible you know.
I read all the information that evening and truth is I'm really keen to find out more. The bottom line is I think I've finally found it. All those years of searching through the small ads has paid off. I'm just so excited I can't contain myself, don't ask me why because at this moment in time all I know is that this is it, I can feel it rushing through my veins! Heck! Why didn't I find this five years ago? Why didn't I find this *ten years ago*? Oh well, better late than never.

That meeting has changed my life. Yes I *know* you've heard that before and you'll probably hear it an awful lot more. Truth is you see, that when people get involved in Network marketing their lives *do* begin to change, all of a sudden there's a real sense of excitement – a light at the end of the tunnel and you'll hear people say it time and time again. Maybe it's because they've reached that point in their lives when it's all or nothing. Time to really look at what the future holds. Pretty scary stuff I can tell you.

The Phone rang, it was John,
"Come to a Jonathan Day"
"Who's Jonathan?"
"It's a national training day, sort of a convention – come you'll enjoy it, It's this Saturday – Birmingham".
I panicked. Visions of tribal warfare entered my mind - of ritual chanting and no escape route, of middle aged boring people with nothing better to do. Hang on a minute *I'm* middle aged (whatever that means) Actually I'm in the prime of life, women who reach 40 are only just beginning to live - we're at our best you see and life is just starting.
In haste I agreed, though to be honest the thought of legging it up to be in Birmingham by 9.30 on a Saturday morning seemed, well just totally

crackers – I'm still cautious you see. Plus I've got heaps of other stuff to do. I've got this weird feeling, can't describe it really, but it's a gut feeling that this is good.

I made the commitment and two days later struggled sleepily out of bed at some unmentionable hour, and hiked it up there (there being somewhere off the M40 near Birmingham) everything a flutter and with mixed feelings. I really didn't know what to expect and to be honest having made the commitment I had to follow through. And so off I went, after all I was a guest. I arrived to the aroma of fresh coffee and a sea of faces. A crowd of happy smiling people, bustling around, a warmth and friendliness that quite honestly made me feel special. It blew me away. Totally. I simply wasn't prepared to see eight hundred people in a room, all having such a brilliant time, all well turned out in their business clothes, and what's this? so many men! (Hmm, I thought this was a ladies only thing, you know, health and nutrition and all of that. How wrong can a woman be?) Was this some sort of cult? Who *are* these people? So there I was. A lamb in the lions den. With no escape route. But actually it wasn't how I thought it would be (how *did* I think it would be?) John sat me down on the very front row so I did feel incredibly special (he whispered in my ear "all the money is made on the front rows. No wonder everyone was scrambling to get to the front.) I sat back not knowing what to expect. Five hours of music, laughter, energy, motivation. It was all there. I was introduced to a heap of really nice people and to Jayne Leach, who to this day together with John have made our world so special. To say I was dumbfounded is the understatement of the year. This was a day where people got on stage and were recognised for their efforts, ordinary folk, people with no special skill sets, but all special for what they had achieved and who they were: a farmer, a panel beater, a teacher, a vet. It was a day full of motivation and a day of surprises. I have to admit I was a bit out of my comfort zone but not for long, heck in for a penny in for a pound, if they can get up and clap so can I! This is great! It's true what they say about network marketing, it just gets into your veins! And gosh I'm a pro so I should know!

Five hours later hungry and high, I floated home. I was sold: totally completely and utterly. This was for me, yep, something definitely was in the air...
I arrived home in a whirr and a flurry to say the least, having flown all down the motorway with the music turned up high and me singing my

head off. What *have* I got my hands on? I don't know and I don't care, I just know it's for me.

That day I was so totally fired up I was uncontainable, like a champagne bottle with the cork pulled, pouring out of the top, unstoppable. I want to tell Robert everything, but I just have this feeling it won't come out right, he *just had* to be there to feel it, experience the whole thing, it's just going to fall flat. I've been exposed to all this fantastic stuff and he's been stuck working at home so how can I possibly relay all those fabulous feelings? Of course It could be just another flash in the pan and to be honest I've tried some of these things before, and they just haven't worked and then I've had to fess up that maybe it wasn't such a good idea after all. So I played it down, gave him the bare essentials, told him I was excited and well, let's just wait and see.. Truth is I'm like a kid in a candy store, just breathless with excitement!

That night my mind was in a spin and I couldn't sleep at all. I had so many questions, so many thoughts...I'm a bit like a butterfly you know, my mind just sort of flutters around from one thing to another and doesn't settle still for one moment, terribly distracting at times, particularly at two a.m. And extremely irritating for those that live with you. I had to get up in the end and make myself some tea and reflect on the past forty-eight hours. I was wide-awake and ready to get things moving.

At the Jonathan day I made my mind up that this was for me. I couldn't wait to meet up with John and fill out the paperwork. I wanted the bottom line "how much is this going to cost me and what do I have to do?" When I realised that in fact I wasn't under any obligation to buy *anything* unless I wanted to, I relaxed (I had horrible visions again of a garage full of products), and the fact that I could return any products I wanted to try and have ninety days to do it in, made it more of a viable proposition. I mean what did I have to lose? Only time in finding out more.

I'm going for it - excited, happy and anxious to get started.

The next step is for me to get the kit, buy the box, the "Combi" try the products whatever – after all I have to know what I'm getting into so I've done just that, completed a registration form and bought the business in a box, what can I say? I'm impatient to get started. Let's get on with it I don't want to waste any more time! I have a choice: It's either go slow, boring and painful, buy stuff one month at a time and never get anywhere, or somehow find the money to buy the essential things you needed to get going. Of course I knew that I would have to buy some of the product if I was serious, but there's always this feeling when you don't know much about anything about how much it's going to cost you long term. Anyway I've decided to go the fast, painful and exciting route. I don't have the money, but I know in my heart I have to go for it, I can see the opportunity and I want it badly. The old plastic came out in amongst cappuccino and toasted teacake that early morning in the Little Chef, and it seemed to work again (how did that happen?) All of a sudden I am all of a flutter and I can't wait to get started.

Now all I have to do is wait for my box of goodies to arrive tomorrow. Today, January 18th I'm officially an "independent distributor", (it's also Robert's birthday how uncanny is that?) working for myself but under the umbrella of this huge successful company, and John and Jayne are my sponsors (because they are now re*spons*ible for me) or upline as they are upline to me.

My philosophy is if you want it badly enough and you feel in your heart it is right – go for it and you will succeed because of your attitude.

Wednesday: It's arrived! This huge box and in it my combi. Can't wait to get in and start trying all this stuff! I'm so fired up I've emptied it now and got all the lotions and potions all around the house to try - including in the kids bathroom (that should be a real test). Oh and I've stuck the two bottles of this jungle juice in the fridge, I have to say its going to take a while to get used to, and Robert has no interest at all in participating, but that's ok he'll come round (hopefully).

I've decided to call my business Dream Team International. Watch out world here I come!

The first few weeks are a bit of a blur, I've got a ton of information that I want to read, So much stuff to get my head around but all done at my own speed, in my own time. trouble is that it's like adding fuel to the fire, I've got a taste and boy I'm hungry for it all, I want it here, now, today! And the days are just flying by because my world has suddenly turned upside down and doing back flips so I can't keep up with it all, so I'll have to give a synopsis on what's been happening.

Diary of A Network Marketer

This first month I'm just reading and reading, most of it all going over my head., but it's incredibly interesting. I was given suggested reading by Jayne and I was an eager student. What is it Jayne said? Oh yes "Readers are leaders and leaders are readers". All this jargon oh and by the way MLM or Multi Level marketing is the same as Network Marketing (in case you wanted to know).

I also went to my first Business Briefing, well actually it's just a friendly meeting (but very professional I hasten to add) when some of the people get together and bring along guests to check out the opportunity.
And what about these meetings? What meetings I can hear you ask? My heart sank when I heard those words. "I just don't have time to go swanning off to meetings in the evening, plus I'm too tired and far too busy". I really wasn't into weekly getting togethers but I've decided that if I intend being successful then I have to make the effort so along I went and now I try and go every week though I don't always make it because inevitably something else crops up last minute. It's really good actually because I recognise some of the people there now and I get all fired up again when I go. At the business briefings they talk about the opportunity and go through the profile of the company and I'm beginning to realise that if I do go every week I'll learn a lot quicker. But one of the most inspiring things is that I am meeting so many decent people. People who genuinely are interested in who I am, and want to help me, it's fantastic! The other great thing about these business briefings is that you realise that everyone else is like you, normal, well sort of. I mean there are all sorts of people there from bankers to dog minders, lorry drivers to PA's. domestic engineers to teachers, doctors to economists, the lot and they all have come into the business for different reasons. My social world is suddenly starting to take a turn for the better.

Network Marketers it seems are naturally friendly, warm folk willing to listen and give you a ton of support, and I am starting to understand that my sponsors will be the ones that will work closely with me, more importantly they will help both of us reach our dreams. And I have oh so many dreams...

NOW WHAT DO I DO?

So what advice can I pass on in this short time that I have got my feet barely wet? Well obviously not a lot. But hey are you impressed with what I've picked up already (I am!) And what about you? Are you sitting now proudly with your combi? well get stuck in! Don't hang around waiting for it all to happen, *make* it happen! How? Ask your sponsor (the person who got you involved) to take you through the first stages. Start your training.

I'm familiarising myself with all the products, got them all around the house and drinking that wicked juice. And I'm reading tons and asking lots of questions. In order to get things going in an upward direction and moving forward I've decided the best line of attack is not to wait for people to call me. I'm going to call them. I'm too impatient anyway. They say Network Marketers don't hang around. That's what I'm doing, I can't wait all day. This business is for me! I want to get on with my life. In letting my sponsor know I'm serious about this I'm finding that they are devoting time and energy with me.

Another thing I'm learning is that to be successful in network marketing, you've got to love the products, and love the industry - live and breathe it, believe in it heart body and soul, be *passionate* about it, but guess what? that doesn't seem to happen straight away, how can it when you've only just got started? I'm taking time out to try it all and getting my family using the products too to see what they think.

Wednesday..
I Went to Fast Start Training last night. It was excellent because it helped me understand a little more of what I've got my hands on. Fast start training is part of the cycle that everyone must go to. It's great because you get to start on the learning curve, plus it gave me the chance to go and check out the centre. It's an hours drive each way but I am keen to learn and understand it is the way forward. I'm beginning to understand how important it is to follow the FLP cycle and how simple it all can be. I also now sort of understand the marketing plan but it's so complicated I don't think I will ever be able to explain it to anyone.

I'M ALL FIRED UP

I'm very fortunate that Rob is behind me all the way and gives me so much help and support in everything I do, and this is no exception, but a few people I've spoken who are new like me, are saying that their spouses/partners are really sceptical and unsupportive when they get involved. I can sort of understand why, I guess it boils down to not knowing enough about how it all works, and not having all the information. Fear conjures up pictures of having garages full of stuff you have to sell – plus *excuse me* but just who *is* this woman that keeps phoning you that you are on first name terms with? Pretty scary stuff. And it just *has* to be pyramid selling? Yeah. But for me it's different, I'm lucky. I've got the full support of my family and that makes my life so much easier. I met this girl last week and she was having such a tough time at home with her spouse, so I suggested (with all my worldly knowledge) that she tread carefully and let him grow into the business in his own time, keeping him informed of what's going on but letting him know she is taking it step by step. Who knows? At the moment it's the blind leading the blind but seems to make sense to me. I mean this is real life. Maybe, (I said), if he came along to the Jonathan Day he'll see the bigger picture, expose him to a room of professional people, all having a ton of fun, it's infectious and motivating and can't help but inspire even the most sceptical of partners. There he can see for himself what a professional company it is and hear ordinary people talking about their success. So I said very informatively parrot fashion: *It's time to decide whether this business is for you, remember: these are your dreams and nothing and no one is going to stop you from reaching your goals.* I'm getting quite good at this...
And no it's NOT PYRAMID SELLING!

OF DREAMING AND DREAMSHEETS

I want it all to happen and now – not tomorrow, not next month, today! What can I say? I'm impatient. Hang on, slow down, step by step, little bits at a time. And so we sat down Jayne and I, at my first business planning around my kitchen table to plan my business - what did I need, *when* did I need it, what were my dreams? It was fun, my mind opened up and I began to dream big time, all the things I have always dreamt. It was magical. Kind of like winning the lottery in my mind. But it all seemed too far away to be real. I was sent away to go and stick and paste, collect all the things I really wanted and put them on paper. I had to do my

"Dream sheet" (Hmm, that sounds sexy!) And I had heaps of fun doing it. When I had finished not only did I have a folder with drop dead goodies on - I plastered my fridge with fabulous oceans and wonderful super yachts so that everyone knows what I'm working towards and they can get excited too. (I left off Tom Cruise.) Of course right now they don't believe it, but it will happen - I have said so. I've got all sorts of stuff on it: a photo of Robert sailing (because he had to sell his boat in the States so I want to buy him another one), oh and a beautiful hotel in Mauritius (Le Geran where all the celebs go) because I've always wanted to go there and learn to scuba dive (hate water and being eaten alive by man eating-sharks I get claustrophobic - not that the two are related). A Camargue 44 (that's a rather deluxe 44 foot power boat with all the bells and whistles currently running at a mere two hundred and fifty thousand pounds that I saw at the boat show this year that I'm going to moor down by Cap D'Ail near Monte Carlo, so that I can cruise around the Med with my chums. A photo of Concorde (well that was before Paris) but I still want to travel first class as I have an intrepid fear of flying (I feel safer in first class), and that's just the beginning, not including all the stuff I want to achieve on the compensation plan. *And* I hasten to add all the good stuff I want to do for homeless children and other charities, but that goes without saying doesn't it..

APPROACHING THE FEAR ZONE: WARM LISTS, and woosies

Today I've been given a rather daunting task to do. I have to draw up a list of people who might want the opportunity: My "Warm" list. Hmm now what about this warm list? Not sure about this. I really don't enjoy the prospect of having to phone all my friends, I think they might be sceptical. Never mind think – I *know* they will be. But anyway I've decided that I shall do as I'm told, because if it has worked for others it has to work for me, and they still have friends (don't they?). No use trying to reinvent the wheel as they say. So we sat down (Jayne and I, again) for a short time and started on it, and I emptied my brain of everyone I knew, all fifty of them. Actually it became a bit of a challenge and it wasn't too long before I started to dig people out of the woodwork. Once I started on this tack I found names popping up all over the place and now I'm waking in the middle of the night and suddenly remembering someone else that needs to go on my list. It's hugely irritating at 3.a.m.

WHAT KIND OF PEOPLE?

What do you mean by what kind of people? Well who exactly do you want in your business? Right now as far as I'm concerned it's anyone or everyone who signs on the dotted line (she said gleefully!) Heck I don't care just fill this part out and leave the rest to me! But actually on reflection maybe it should be people who are motivated. People who are willing to take action themselves – Why? Well for one thing Jayne has said it will be less hard work. I guess I do *genuinely* want people who are excited after all it is my business at the end of the day. I don't want to end up mothering them and holding their hand, I need them to take their own action under guidance, otherwise I'll be dragging them over the finishing line instead of them racing ahead. I don't want the sort of people that are boring (you know the kind) the ones that sit there and don't contribute to the conversation, the type that always have a negative outlook on life, The ones that always have excuses. Plus I'm so incredibly impatient I need people who can see things clearly. Whatever happens I know that I mustn't try to manipulate, convince or persuade them, because if *they* are not convinced and motivated, they'll just drop out later, disappear in a heartbeat and I'll have wasted so much time. I'm going to show them the opportunity and let *them* make the decision, let them really want it and come back all fired up and raring to go (that's the plan anyway) right now though anyone who shows any interest is an angel from heaven! I have to make them realise that this is a fantastic chance for them to make a difference in their lives and that of others and then walk away and let them stew on that for a while. Dangle the carrot...

I've been told too that it's important not to discriminate at this point, writing out your warm list is simply an exercise to get your brain into gear. Who are we after all to judge who needs this business and who doesn't? Just because someone has a fab house and a Merc in the drive doesn't necessarily mean that they are loaded, hey they could be up to their ears in debt (probably are). Nor should we *not* offer the opportunity to people who we think don't have the necessary skills – there are individuals who I would never have put on my list who have done incredibly well and on their way to their goals especially to our friends when you want to offer them a fantastic opportunity should be relatively easy right? Mmm well yes in theory.. After all, here I am offering the chance of a lifetime to work from home, part time, and earn tons of money – so why am I getting so hung up over it all? Well I guess its because I'm having to get out of my comfort zone. And then there's this whole rejection thing. It's the fear of them saying "You're doing what? Are you *totally mad*? Oh Pyramid selling – no thanks!" and all the other million and one negative things. Oops! Did I hit a nerve?

But if you are shown from the start the *right* way to talk to your friends, how to offer the opportunity, you will end up with more maybes and yes's than no's. And guess what? That's the biggest motivation in the whole world! What so impresses me is all the help and support I'm getting. I certainly never expected it, and although this is my business everyone is being so great in helping me identify what I want out of life and how to get there. I've really got to get out of my comfort zone here and pick up the phone, this is my future after all. I've discovered a truly incredible company. What *have* I got my hands on...?

I'm in control. Well, sort of. ...

BACK TO BASICS: STUFF I NEED TO GET STARTED

So what did I need that first month in order to get started apart from tons of ambition, attitude, motivation and action? Well here's a list:

A kitchen table. My kitchen tables' great, it's covered in old paint stains from my painting days, and it's kind of got a real warm feeling to it. I'm not saying you have to work from your kitchen table, hey you may not have one, but it works for me! Other things that I found I needed are a computer (if you are really going to get serious), envelopes, paper, a printer, oh and telephone. A pad of paper, pen and calendar and diary. A 6 x 2 card file box with index cards with days of the month on and half a dozen files. And that's it! I'm not the tidiest person in the world and it's become quite a challenge keeping things in order. On top of that I'm useless at book keeping so at some point some point I know I'm going to be an absolute nightmare to an accountant - oh well.

It's the end of the first crazy month and looking back what would I have done differently? Difficult to say really because I don't know what I'm doing either right or wrong but something must be going ok because it's all starting to happen.

Diary of A Network Marketer

I know it may seem that I'm a mine of information but it's quite amazing what stuff you pick up if you are really interested, actually it's all a bit of a farce because I don't really know what the hell I'm doing..
But hey - it feels good! And all of a sudden I just feel the world is going around the right way!

I love this business!

Tip of the month: Be excited and enthusiastic - people buy *you* before anything else!

FEBRUARY 2000
Of phone calls and flippancy

I've been exactly thirteen days in the business! I know you won't believe it but I have immersed myself in tons of literature and books and just read whenever I can (well that amounts to about ten minutes in bed before lights out or before I fall asleep whichever happens sooner).. I haven't read for years but suddenly I've got this burning desire to ingest all this info, most of it goes over my head and I've forgotten it by the morning but some of it seems to stick.

It's time to get down to the nitty gritty: making phone calls. Yep no getting out of it. For most of us phone calls can be a nightmare, not for me, I'm lucky because I've been doing it most of my life, but still this is different, and I'm a wee bit out of my comfort zone.. So we sat down, my sponsor and I and went through my "warm list" (it's that dreaded warm list again) and identified a few possible people to call, people who I thought would be great in the business, people that really needed a second income.

And so it started…Most of the people on my list I had already decided didn't want the business so that only left a handful but I did have a group of sales reppy people that I thought might be good. (wrong!)

So then we had to make the dreaded phone call.

Are you any good talking to people you know when you really don't know much about what you are trying to say? It's really hard and there's no other option but just to say what they hell and get on with it. So here it is. Jayne asked me to Pick my top ten people and ask myself what their hot button might be.

"What's a hot button?"

"It's what makes them fire up – it's that one thing that gets them going. Maybe it's someone who's in a dead end job, working all hours, shift work, no time with the family, poor pay,. Stressed out, mountain of debt etc. get the picture?"

So I picked someone I knew on my list who was really in dire need of cash and went through my mind with what I was going to say using phrases that Jayne had suggested. I certainly wasn't going to do it there and then (are you crazy!) but I will do it later. General guidelines (I was told) was to make the conversation brief, exciting and to the point! Mmm! Oh and to always ask if now is a good time to call.

> *"Hi Tony, how's things? (General waffle) have you got a minute? I've very recently started a part time business that I think may interest you. I know you are having a rough time at work and working long hours, never any time with the kids, well this is something that can help you have more time with the family – be financially free of debt and work the hours you want – I know it sounds too good to be true – but it's simply amazing and I really would like to tell you about it – are you free tomorrow evening?"*

That's what I was *supposed* to say but of course it wasn't at all like that. I was all over the place with bits thrown in here and there and general waffle added. Somehow or other in all the flurry and excitement I think he got the message enough to say that he would meet up to find out more. How the heck did that happen? I tell you my heart was definitely in mega drive! I really didn't have a clue...

It's Thursday and I am just so excited! I got on the phone, (again) took the bull by the horns, and called up lots of my friends, didn't really know what I was doing or saying at that stage, except I had stumbled across an incredible opportunity and I wanted them to be a part of it. Some of what I said fell on stony ground but I am learning one of the first lessons in network marketing: be prepared for negativity and whatever you *do don't take it personally*. (Ha! Easier said than done my friend!) As they say in the business: some will, some wont so what? Next! Its quite hard when you get lots of "no's" but eventually law of averages says that you will find someone who says yes.
And you do. Trust me, it happens. Might not happen at your speed - but it happens.

I discovered that if I can make my phone calls direct and to the point without getting into too much stuff I don't get bombarded with too many questions I can't answer.. However the next few calls were not quite as successful; actually they were quite disastrous. I was on a roll and started to get flippant and cocky. The biggest pitfall I made was in starting to tell them all about the business there and then on the phone, all about the bees happily buzzing in the desert and the nine hundred and ninety nine ingredients in aloe – let me tell you I was on the phone forever digging myself a deeper hole by the second! By keeping it very short (less than five minutes) and sticking to a script that I had written out for guidance, I came to the conclusion that I could tweak their interest. I didn't want to be secretive or withhold information but was told that if they are overly persistent, I can say something like:

"I'm not trying to withhold information but I simply can't tell you all about a one billion dollar company in five minutes over the phone." It works with most people. "What happens if they can't meet up?" I panicked. Then there's always the option to send them some info in the post on the condition that you can call them in a couple of days to find out what they think, and you can say *"if you like what you see we can take it to the next step and if you don't – we wont is that fair?"*

(I'm quoting here by the way..do you really think I can remember all this stuff at this stage?) Always remember (John said) that at this stage that *all* you are doing is sifting and sorting, offering the opportunity just as you would offer someone a cup of coffee, you wouldn't get bent all out of shape if someone said no to that would you? No I wouldn't. It's really hard to not take a "Not interested" or a "no" personally, bashes the ego somewhat but I'm learning to say thank you and leave the door open *"can I call you in six months to see what your situation is then?"* And to always ask for a referral: *I understand that this might not be for you but who do you know that would like to get rich? Or would like a better lifestyle? Or would like to get out of the rat race? Or would like to work part time from home, be their own boss and be stinking rich and have a mountain of fun?* Ha! could get facetious here!

Back to the phone calls. When I made those first few calls I was like a bull in a china shop (same bull) and everything went out of the window - right out. I was so excited I lost the plot completely - waffled on for ages, but you know what was great? Because I really couldn't explain what I was doing, some of my friends agreed to meet with me, it was fantastic! Looking back I suppose it was that initial enthusiasm that got everyone hooked and it worked! No stopping me now. And there I was, walking around the room arms going everywhere and wearing out the carpet, by

Diary of A Network Marketer

the time I had finished the phone was positively warm with hot breath.. It went something like this:

> *"Hi Amanda, It's me, how are things– is now a good time to call? Listen I've only got a minute because I'm taking the hamster to the vet for an itchy bum but I simply had to ring you! I'm really so excited because I've just started an incredible business opportunity and I thought how great you would be at this. You know how you hate that job of yours, long hours and stressed out – well I think I may have found just the thing for you. I can't tell you about it right now – but can we get together for coffee tomorrow?"*

Guess what? It worked! Not each and every time, but it produced enough interest for people to meet up with me to find out more.

What am I learning these early days? Well my sponsor is a hard taskmaster:

> *"I'd like you to make fifteen phone calls a day"*
> *"What?"* (gasp) (this could be tough when your contact list is only fifty - you soon run out)
> *"What if I don't have time?"*
> *"If you want to have the house, the boat and everything else you'll need to make the time.. If you get organised its only going to take you twenty minutes in the evening. Bottom line is one in ten people will come on board so if you only call one person every other day it's going to be a long haul…"*
> *"What if I can't phone fifteen?"*
> *"At least speak to two people during the day and offer them the opportunity somehow someway – on your way to work, at the newsagents, wherever. Keep info, flyers, business cards, tapes on your body somewhere, in the car, in your wallet so that you always have something to hand out plus I'm going to show you how to expand your contact list - you know loads more people it's just that you haven't put them down yet."*

And we did..
I've gone back to working on my contact list. I've made a huge huge list of people I know, went through all my business cards, address books, diaries, yellow pages, you name it I was pulling them all out of the wood work, there they all were. Some I haven't spoken to in years, some have moved away, but I'm amazed at just how many people I know. It can be a bit

tricky at first making the call if you haven't spoken to someone for a while, so I did the usual: went through the elementary stuff of finding out and catching up etc. And then in for the plunge. Actually most people were quite chuffed that I've thought of them. I ho hummed for a while but eventually got it sort of right.

I've got the phone pitter patter down pat more or less, though each time it's different, but I always keep the phone call short and it seems to be my enthusiasm that gets me meetings. I don't try and make calls when I've had a rotten day, it just doesn't work, people sense my mood even over the phone. Any excuse to have a glass of wine and chill out for the evening and start again another time.

Time for another bag of chocolate buttons..

Let's party! I mean PRODUCT LAUNCHES (Excuse me?)

I am NOT doing parties! There I've said it - no way hose..
It's just not my scene.

So I sat down with Jayne:

"I'm really not happy about this - it really *isn't* my scene at all"

and this is what she said:

> *"In any business there are things that we need to do to get ourselves up and running and this is no different. If it means that you have to do a couple of product launches or business launches call them what you will, then it will serve as a training ground for you, plus you will gain some retail customers".*

I need about ten to twenty retail customers so I suppose one must do what one must do, plus going through the motions will familiarise me with the products. Oh all right then.

It occurred to me later (much later) that although I didn't want to retail big time and do launches, in fact there could be people out there who would love to do it, so I had to step back and look at it from that point of view. And it all begins to make sense.

I made a date in the diary, rang around some of my friends and invited them to come along and support me in my new venture. I invited fifteen people. It was a good excuse for a quick spring clean, I managed to make the living room acceptable, clean and tidy with fresh flowers and a few candles dotted here and there to create some atmosphere. Only eight showed up which is par for the course, and what I expected. I offered them something to drink and some cheesy things that were interesting, and sat and listened. John and Jayne both came to my first product launch and did a brilliant job and I sat there thinking, "I'll never be able to do this!" It was fun except I insisted that they do it my way so naturally we didn't get the result intended. I'm stubborn you know (one of these people that know it all, supposedly). It wasn't a disaster but it could have been better if I had let them do it their way and not mine (that's the salesman in me - or salesperson I should say.) I didn't want them going on about products (big mistake). Anyway not to be deterred I thought maybe I *can* do this, so a few weeks later I held my very own product launch in my own home, scary stuff but it had to be done. I'd been doing a lot of reading about the products and Jayne assured me everything would be OK. And you know what? It wasn't so bad. I felt it was time for me to launch out on my own, heck it couldn't be that difficult could it? So I phoned around some of the people who didn't make the last one, plus knocked on a few doors in the neighbourhood of people I knew. It was a case again of come and support me and no you don't have to buy anything - just be there.

I called the evening before to remind them, and said "don't forget tomorrow night" that way they couldn't wiggle out (some did anyway). I invited ten and six showed up. And yes I was nervous when I started out. My mind went completely blank (as it does), but then I remembered that they really didn't know what I was talking about, and so long as I didn't lie I could waffle through it all, which I did, and it went OK. I think everyone found it interesting (either that or they were faking it), plus between them they spent two hundred pounds, so I was thrilled to pieces – hey I can do this! I made about sixty pounds, not bad for a fun evening in! I was on such a buzz that I did another one a few weeks later but couldn't be bothered to phone around to remind everyone and consequently no one came. I was mortified - how dare they! I sat waiting and waiting watching the clock and not a soul. What had I done wrong?

Big lesson to be learnt here: ALWAYS, always make sure to phone people up the *night before* and remind them. Forget remind them, *insist* they have to be there - it's do or die!

The thought of having a product launch or whatever you want to call them brings back memories of the seventies and Tupperware, Avon and Anne Summers. (Have you ever been to an Anne Summer's party? Neither have I). The fear zone sets in and it's the last thing on earth I wanted to do. But the great thing about product launches is that it is a good training ground. I've got to get to know the products really well so what better way than to be with a group of friends. I know it doesn't matter if I don't really know it all, I won't anyway, and yes I'll screw up and make mistakes – but that's ok it's all about learning and once I've done one I'll be off! The other thing about product launches is that I can immediately start to make money. There will always be someone there who will buy (even if it's out of pity watching me struggle through) and I'll slowly build up a customer base.

As I become confident and savvy about all of this I am sure I will sail through these evenings and become better. In the meantime, for every person who bought something during the course of the evening I made up a customer record card, (this is what the index box is for). I wrote down their name, address, telephone number, date, the products they bought and any relevant info (the reason they may have bought the product). As the products are consumable it goes without saying that people run out so it's a good way of keeping track and I've got a dreadful memory. Looking after customers is key. It shows you care. I might only have ten, but I will phone them regularly and see how they are getting on with the products and what new ones they would like to try.

"What if I have people who insist that they won't do product launches" I wailed? It's not the end of the day. It just will take a while longer because instead of having a captive audience it means having to go around person to person, just like going around the ring road instead of through the town –that's all.

It's getting out of my comfort zone time (again?) Ahh!!
Get confident!

But product launches are only a beginning, a training ground, a way to build a customer base. I need to get down to the *real* business. **The art of duplication.** (Key words here, so I'll repeat them: **the art of duplication**.). Now I do need to really make things happen, to start getting people in my business because in all truthfulness this is what really gets the ground shaking. Apart from having a red-hot lover.

Throughout all this time I keep regularly in contact with John and Jayne, in fact I phone them everyday because I'm just so excited! How great to have someone believe in you!
God I hope my new distributors don't phone me at 8.30 every morning...

IT WORKS! FINALLY!
I'm having a lie down.
My first yes came in the form of my dear friend Sam. Mine Gott! I was on cloud one hundred and ninety nine! I have a fairy Godmother after all.. My first recruit! My first team (all one of them!) I feel just fab, I've done it, conquered the world, no stopping me now! It was in fact quite easy, I had most of the info I needed to do a sort of half baked presentation and it obviously worked which proves a point that you really don't have to be the bees knees and all of that straight off. It all came about with the phone call and me saying how's about doing your own thing, earning some money etc. etc.? Mmm seemed like a great idea (by the way they are not all this easy in fact 80 % of them are blooming hard work!) Sam was a PA, lived actually a very nice lifestyle and didn't really need the money. Was always down at House of Frazer shopping but I discovered her hot button was not so much the money, but self-development, being in control, running the show – perfect. There we were the three of us, me Sam and John and we showed her the business opportunity. Lots of questions and answers later she said yes this sounded great! I can't tell you what a sense of excitement I have – I'm just bouncing around. Wow! That was easy! So we left her some info on the company and the products – ordered some products for her to try, and set a date in the diary for when we could plan her business. We made the appointment for a few days later because we were all hot to trot and we wanted to get things up and running. At the next meeting, we made a business plan the purpose of which was to find out how much did she want to earn and in what time frame? Then there was the issue of self-development, how

Diary of A Network Marketer

could we achieve that? We also got her started on her own personal dream sheet, after all, without dreams you cannot build a business – simple as that. And then we got to work, gave her a list of things to do that week go to training, talk to people, and have a couple of product launches. I'm on a high and having endless sleepless nights on how to move things along at a greater speed

Monday:
I've got into the habit of making numerous phone calls each day (well it seems numerous in reality it's probably about five) and the net result is I've got someone else interested in coming along to a business briefing. Things are looking good and the adrenaline is definitely pumping - hey this beats running any day! Amanda's an aromatherapist, always out on full throttle. Well she just needs the business doesn't she? let's face it she won't get the house in Portugal at the speed she is going so I'm really excited about telling her more. I'll let you know after tomorrow..

Wednesday:
Forget Tuesday it was too late to let you know the outcome so I'll fill you in. We went along to the meeting - and now I'm getting to know a few people it's really cool, and I sat Amanda down on the front row at the end so she couldn't escape without tripping over everyone else which would cause huge embarrassment.

I'm getting to learn quite a lot about the company when I go to the meetings, plus there's always such a buzz at the meetings it's great to participate. Afterwards we went to check out the products and I introduced her to a couple of people that I have met. I think this may really be for her, she's giving me the signs anyway. (Either that or she is really good at faking it).

Friday:
I've been really good and done the follow up call expecting the brush off but no - Amanda's in for the ride and I am just tickety boo! So we've planned to go to the Fast start training and then a business plan and then hopefully it will all fall into place.

Synopsis: without wishing to sound like Bridget Jones diary (hate that book) I'll fill in the gaps - bottom line I've got a new distributor who is just so excited there is no stopping her, she's rushed out, got product

31

Diary of A Network Marketer

launches the whole nine yards. Great, I'm leaping for joy, she wants it as badly as me. And I know she will be a superstar!

Two weeks later:
Jayne is helping me with one to ones as I still don't have a clue how to do all the numbers, but now it's time for me to step out and do some product launches on my own.. So it's off to Amanda's we go. No mean feat as she doesn't live on the doorstep, and I'm still new at all of this, so making heaps of mistakes, but hey this is my business and nothing's too much effort.

The first launch only three people turned up - disappointing. Even worse, the second launch, the one I was supposed to do the following week *no one turned up!*
" What went wrong?" I asked? (This is still the case of the blind leading the blind though I am getting the hang of things sort of..)

She had made the carnal sin of not following through and reminding people - oh well. Undeterred, we shrugged it off as a learning curve, and resolved to still build a customer base of finding ten people who might like to try the products by trying again and getting our act together and we finally succeeded by having a successful launch. But it doesn't always happen like that I hasten to add..

A few days later I then had a chance meeting with an old work colleague and put the question:

"So how about some extra cash at the end of the month?"

Pennies from heaven! It took three meetings but Dan signed up. And then there were three. So the three of us carried on. That same month Dan got his brother in law involved. Funnily he didn't want to phone him for ages. Kept saying

"He won't want this – He's far too busy"
"Oh for goodness sake just get on and make the phone call and then at least you can cross him off" I said.

Diary of A Network Marketer

Well Andy turned around and simply said *"Why didn't you phone me 6 weeks ago – I've been looking for something like this to let me be able to give up work and have more time with the kids".* You see, you *just don't know.*

So I've started duplicating! What's duplicating? It's the stuff network marketing is made of, it's what has to happen if you want a really successful business, it's the stuff dreams are made of, it's no good simply having tons of people retailing the product (though that's a good idea too' obviously product has to be moved) but getting other people to do the same as you: build a team.

So far I've been on product training, network training and business briefings, all in the first six weeks. I'm doing around seven to ten hours a week, (alongside my full time business) which consists of going to training's and meetings and the occasional presentation. I've also learnt how to put in an order and I'm slowly starting to get the hang of a few things. I've ordered some business cards because I never have anything to give anyone and it looks really good!

I've approached the local pet shop to see if they would like to offer the products to their customers via the database (because he can't display the products on the shop floor - that would upset loads of people and I would be in the dog house (ha - pun!)) and Jeff the pet man is thinking about it, he quite likes the idea so I will work on that.

I've put in a new phone line and got myself organised.

Who else? Oh yes then there's Hattie. Hattie isn't exactly my type, I mean I can't see us really as pals but that isn't what this is about, plus she always insists that she is right all the time – I don't exactly embellish the idea of having her in my group but at this point everyone is an opportunity. Like all decent people I have given her the benefit of the doubt and now realise that I was right all along (see you get to be good at this later on) She's negative. And a wimp – sorry. Negative the whole time but still wants to do it (Mmm?) She had a product launch and still knocked the products – still don't quite understand that one either, anyway she quit literally days after she signed up, but that's how it goes sometimes. Some people just don't get it do they? She lasted all of five minutes.

33

Diary of A Network Marketer

And what about Yvonne? I got really excited about Yvonne because she was just all over the place about the business. I mean if it was for anyone it *had* to be for her she was perfect. She had it all planned and sort of knew what she wanted for her goals but never wrote them down it was all "in her head". She's bought the combi, and likes the products but doesn't do anything else because she's always too busy. So what was so exciting a few weeks ago has fizzled out and I just can't get her motivated to do anything - the urgency has gone and I'm so frustrated I just want to grab her by the lapels and say "*wake up you're missing the whole thing!*"

So who's left after this first month? Well, Sam of course because I won't let her quit and besides that she's too fired up about it all and five others so I really am quite proud of myself. And the others that bailed out? Well they lost the plot. I suppose there are those that will have a go at it but for whatever reason, the time isn't right, or maybe they just aren't the right people? I know now, looking back that really they weren't the sort of people who would truly make a go of it, too much other stuff going on in their lives. So I'm learning a lot, and yes it really hurts when you've spent time (and money travelling) on people and then they bail out later. But better now than in a year from now (imagine how much *more* time and money you would have spent).

So what have I learnt? Be upfront with people, ask them if they will be committed to reach their dreams, let them know you will give them all the support they need and won't let them fail but you need that commitment from them. It's hard because I so desperately want to recruit people, but I'm beginning to understand that I need to be somewhat selective and I've got to let people know from the getko that this is a serious (but fun) business – yes, I'll help them reach their dreams but they must be teachable.

I've got this friend, Debbie – God she would be so perfect for this, anyway..

My daughter left for skiing today and sent me a text message from the coach saying she wanted to come home (wouldn't you after twenty-four hours on a stinky coach full of obnoxious teenagers?) I'm so miserable, I just want to pick her up and give her a hug.

People signed up this month: 6 (wow how did I do that?)

Diary of A Network Marketer

Training's attended: 3

Phone calls: masses – at least 10 a day! (that could be a slight exaggeration)

Books read: 3: "Being the Best you can be" (John Kalench), "Your first year in Network Marketing" (Yarnell) & "Attitude is everything" Jeff Keller

Tapes: Building a network marketing Business (Jim Rohn)

Meetings: 3

Dropouts: 2

People spoken to: Around 70 My first cheque's arrived, smack on time, gosh I'm so excited £57! I've taken a copy of it and stuck it in a file for future reference and I'm going to set up a separate bank account. From now on everything to do with the business will go into that account and I've decided that 10% of everything I earn is going to be put away into another separate account, a nest egg that will grow. I haven't bothered with getting my taxes etc. sorted out at this stage, I'll do that later when the bigger cheques start rolling in!

What a long month this has been!

Oh and I went to a TNT training. What's that I hear you ask? Well it's an invite from HQ on "Top Networker Training". Pretty good I can tell you. First you get to look around the fabulous offices at Longbridge Manor which are very impressive - lots of lovely polished wood and very old. And you get to meet all the staff. Then you have a whole day of really excellent training. I had such a fun time and got to meet some very nice people. I came home simply buzzing and totally worn out. It all makes sense now.. well most of it.

What would I have done differently? Talked to people at every opportunity even those I thought wouldn't have been interested
Even though I really didn't know what I was talking about.

Tip of the month? Be confident - Read and learn all you can about the company, the products, the opportunity and the industry.. It will pay you back tenfold...

MARCH 2000
Help! My warm list's run out!

What do you mean your warm list has run out? You're supposed to work on that for *at least* six months according to the oracle, and the oracle knows. Actually you're supposed to work on it *forever*. Well let me tell you sunshine, mine's well and truly done and dusted (actually there are people on there that I still haven't rung and don't want to ring so I've left it alone). What do you do when you've run out of people to call?

Well there's always the COLD MARKET (the rest of the world) that's even scarier than the warm market. How? Well, I've begun putting small ads in shop windows, I don't want to do newspaper advertising just yet as it costs an arm and a leg around here. I've also thrown together some flyers to give out at trade fairs. I've started to go to the health clubs and centres and ask if I can put flyers up, and most of them don't mind. I ran through some of the stuff with my sponsor because there is so much you cannot say (you have to be careful with the wording on the flyers.)

I'm getting a pro at this. I have found that I can talk to people now more easily about the opportunity. I'm doing my own one to ones, (however I still take my calculator for the numbers.) I've started to overcome the fear bit because I have such strong beliefs. I simply know that I am going to get there come what may and nothing is going to get in my way.

And guess what? It's all paying off all these phone calls because the long and the short of it is that this month they are all falling over me, incredible (it can't last!) so at the moment I am flying! I still think it's because I am just overflowing with enthusiasm, must be. Anyway I've got them all hot to trot and people coming on board like there is no tomorrow! I've signed up three people already this month and still ten days to go so I guess I'm doing something right!

Someone said to me recently that Network Marketing is like a rollercoaster ride. You're telling me sunshine, one minute it's all hunky dory and the next it's all downhill. Mmm, I guess I see what they mean now because Amanda didn't last the course, her enthusiasm died when she stopped trying. She didn't go on the training and didn't follow up on her customers. I couldn't believe that with all her enthusiasm she would

37

quit and go back to her aromatherapy but she did, and you know what? Looking back the timing wasn't right for her, but I didn't realise that at the time. I'm new at this game after all.
Hell, all that petrol I wasted...

Plus there's all the "No shows". You know the people that say yep they are going to be at the business briefings, and you hang around like a dead duck nervously waiting and they don't show. What *is* it with people, can't they pick up the phone and make a phone call? I guess not!

I'm doing more hours in the business, probably around ten to twelve hours a week and I'm having so much fun to be honest it just doesn't seem like hard work. I snatch twenty minutes here and there, and yes there are times when I get totally hacked off. People dismissing me, telling me it's pyramid selling, people who just don't want to know, reeking of scepticism, but the more confident I become the more it just washes over me. I've developed an attitude that if they don't want it, it's their loss; I'm not going to persuade them, I just will move on and speak to someone else. And you know what? If I speak to five people who put me down I just carry on until I find someone who listens, and if I still don't find anyone I call my sponsor, tell them I'm getting totally demoralised and miserable and they always make me feel good again. There's always a way believe me.

I regularly attend meetings and trainings. Go out on wet and cold nights and travel for an hour to get there, but I know it's worth it and has to be done. Every time I go up to the monthly meetings in Birmingham the great Jonathan days (all two of them) I buy one or two books and a tape. I soak up all the information I can and read like an eager beaver for ten minutes every night before bed. I've got tapes in the car, and I listen to them at every opportunity, they are so motivational! And I make notes when I go to trainings all the time, and write them out again later for future reference on the computer and copy them for my group. But above all I talk to my sponsors and I ask them how to do it, how to be the best I can be, show me just how, and I'll do it.

My dreamsheet has expanded. I sent off for Luxury destinations of the world (in fact I asked the travel agent to send me ten copies so that I can give them out to my new people) and I've cut out the hotel I want to stay at in Mauritius at two thousand pounds per person per week. The interesting thing is that in this short time I've changed the goal posts: I won't wait to get Rob out of his job in five years, it's going to be in twelve months time, that means hard graft! Still not sure if it's going to happen, but if I work at it will! Christmas 2001 – that's the goal, no mean feat I can tell you. Kids are still great, still behind me and using the products and guess what, liking them! My daughter getting positive results, and don't forget these are young adults (eighteen and twenty) so they are the first to let you know if you are barking up the wrong tree! And I so desperately, desperately want them to have the good things in life, time to enjoy themselves, freedom, choice.

I think I'm going to get to Supervisor on the compensation plan this month. Well it's the next step on the marketing plan. I'm so excited I can't contain myself! My pay cheque is slowly on the up and up. I guess that's the hardest bit really – working hard and not being able to reap the financial rewards, not yet anyway but I know that all I am doing right now is sowing the seeds and finding my people and getting them on the straight and narrow.

I'm still trying so hard to get the local pet shop on board he is so stubborn, boy what a market he has! Anyway he has bought a few of the products but the timing isn't right for him at the moment. Maybe it never will be who knows?

Do you know I go to bed some nights and my head is just spinning around and around and I have to get up and write stuff down in case I forget.

Cheque this month: £167.67
Retail: £200
People signed up: 6 (again!)
People spoken to: loads
Trainings: some
Product launches: Yes
Dropouts: a few
Books read: "Success Happens" (Tom Barret), "Wave 3" Richard Poe, "Dare to Dream work to win" (Tom Barrett - again)
Tapes: "How to build a giant heap" Kim Klaver

Some nice kind person I met at a meeting gave me a really cute badge that says: "I make money, ask me how", It's so great I've gone and got some more and given them out to my team to wear. When someone stops to ask me what it's all about I tell them I have an incredible business opportunity and I'm looking for five key people who want to work from home. If they seem interested, I give them a tape which briefly tells them about the business opportunity and the company, get their address and phone number (in my little book) and tell them I'll be calling them in a couple of days to see what they think.

Gosh this stuff is so easy sometimes! (But not always!)

So what would I have done differently this month? Followed up on people a lot quicker – not left it a week by which time they've lost interest.

Tip of the month: Take action every single day - and don't blame your team if you have a bad month - it's down to you!

APRIL
Snow, sun, sex and Chamonix!

Not necessarily in that order but I've decided that to wash away the winter blues it's time to have time out – so as a belated birthday present to my other half and a treat for me (well he needed someone to go with) off we are going into the blue and beyond….

Chamonix is just delightful and we stayed at this brilliant pine chalet which overlooked Mont Blanc – what a view to wake to! Plus we had a chalet girl, wow, what luxury (actually it really didn't break the bank because there were six of us sharing.) This girl was the tops, every morning we rose sleepily to the aroma of freshly baked croissants and then at tea, cold and exhausted from our day on les pistes we came back to home made cakes. In the evening later, much later, and somewhat rested, the day would end with the best gourmet meal served with copious wine AND we didn't have to wash up – I could live like that! Then we sloped off to bed awash with Merlot and the warmth of the fire, and the snow falling softly outside the window…

Bonjour Chérie (I'm practising mon French) où ést le vin? (Trés important) And combien ést the croissant au chocolat? Actually forgettez le prix I'll have three merci..plus numerous rude words that are unrepeatable that I have down pat for strange men that whistle in alleyways when I'm on my own.

The skiing was great, not that I'm a great skier I hasten to add but I do manage to get down more or less in one piece. These days I spend most of the time halfway up the mountain in the bar looking at all the ski buffs in really cool gear; trying to see if anyone interesting might unexpectedly show up; I've heard Pierce Brosnan occasionally hits Chamonix (or was it Tom Cruise?) Anyway not a peek of anyone remotely famous. Dommage. It was bitterly cold. Even with piles of thermals on the cold still manages to seep through all my gear. Plus I was so unfit it was a real shock to the system! Must get back into the gym (fat chance). And it snowed – big time. Don't you just love the snow? I love the snow, lots of it and when it gets really really cold like –20 degrees, and you can come home to a blazing fire and a good bottle of red. I don't do really really cold weather, when it's so cold your fingers drop off and it takes hours to warm up even when you get into the warm.. *And,* can you believe it, someone we went with (who's now in my group and shall be nameless!) decided to sneak a day in earlier just to get on the slopes and fell down a pothole and broke her ankle before we had even arrived. Ha! Shame on you! Though I must admit I did feel terrible that we were off swanning on les pistes and she had to sit and watch halfway up the mountain. Oh well. One week of bliss and then, oh yes back to the real world, if only we could have more hols like that – but we *can* I hear this voice saying in my ear, just wait and see!

One of my team quit this month. Dan the man actually. such a blow because he's so great and would be really good, at least I think he would, plus he's got some really good contacts. But at least I got his list off him so now I can call them up. How did I do that? Well I just said:

"You don't know me, my names blah blah, but xxx has told me that you are a really excellent communicator (or whatever) and I am looking for a few good people to join me working part time from home without compromising their job? Can I send you some info?"

Flattery works wonders! (without going overboard naturally). Anyway Dan worked in a car manufacturing company and for a whole month he followed the FLP system. Problem was there was an issue at home, you know the one where the other half just doesn't want to know and gives a hard time. I believe they ended up in separate beds (how terrible). Ironically, in the same village another group has set up recently, small world! I did call several times to try and salvage everything to let him hold on to his dreams but alas to no avail he didn't return my calls. I never heard from him again. I hope he will be very happy, sad to think his dreams have come to a grinding halt because of lack of support. Bet the stuff still is sitting in the box. Perhaps one day he'll get it out again when the wife is over it.

Yippee! I've done it! I've made Supervisor, what a sweat it's been at the last minute and I feel, well I just feel over the moon. (Yes I know it means nothing to you but revel in my glory anyway). One day sooner rather than later this will be you too.. I've achieved many things in my life and some in reality would appear to be far more wonderful but do you know this is the best thing that has happened to me in ages and I really feel like I've deserved it! I'm really on the way now!

Diary of A Network Marketer

"SO WHAT EXACTLY DO YOU DO?"

Good question! One of the great things about people asking me what I do is that it opens up the chance for me to tell them about the business of course! But what does "Hi I'm a Network Marketer" mean to the average Jo blo? Probably not a heck of a lot! So what I am starting to say (having got many blank faces over the past few months) is: *"I help people develop second incomes."* Or: *"I'm in Marketing - health and nutrition:* Or if I'm feeling exceptionally cheeky *"I'm a trainee millionaire".* Hey I have all the tools to make people into millionaires! so what if it hasn't happened yet – it will! *"are you a millionaire yet?"* they ask *"ha! Not yet but I'm on my way sunshine!"* Just watch this space, or better still come and join me!

ON BUILDING RELATIONSHIPS

I'm learning swiftly, through reading, training's, and motivational speakers. And making mistakes - of course.

One of the key things that I'm starting to understand is that I need to build relationships with the people I meet. Fundamental stuff you may say but it's so easy to start rabbitting on about the business and not stop and listen. So I'm learning to hang fire. I'm making a real effort to find out about the people I'm talking to, asking them questions, what do they do? What do they want? What's important to them? and most importantly what are their values? In taking the time out to do this I'm finding that people are more receptive, they start to make a bond – people love to talk about themselves so I just give them the opportunity! It's worth its weight in gold! So often we just don't give people enough time to tell us what's important to them and then we miss the show. So now I spend loads of time asking questions and finding out what the real issues are, what they really want, where they want to be. It's all good stuff.

TEAM SPIRIT

I've got a team! Only a mini team, sort of like a mini Christmas cake, all the ingredients in a tiny format (like the ones you see in the bakers). It's such fun! Now I have to develop leadership skills otherwise the whole thing is going to fall apart. Being in a team is quite a challenge, you have to keep all the balls up in the air – unrealistic obviously, but that's the idea. And it really is fun! So now my phone keeps ringing and I get lots of questions some of which I still don't know the answer and probably a lot more to come that I don't know the answer, so I just phone up my sponsor and get the information I need.

Keeping in touch with what people are doing is critical. If I leave it up to them most of them don't do anything, I've got to get them up and motivated so that they do all these things on their own. Go to training, start reading, and following through the system. My confidence is growing and I feel good being able to help them out when they need help. I do phone my team regularly to find out what they are doing, plus I write tons of emails – and we meet every week if possible to plan ahead for the month so that we all know what we are doing. It's really important that I make sure my team calls me weekly just to let me know how they are getting on – and I don't ever, ever forget to praise them when they do well. Recognition is so important in this industry. And FLP is unbelievable in it's recognition for a job well done - how great it feels to get on stage at the Jonathan all a trembling and get your pin - your fifteen seconds of fame! Well it's important full stop. I've learnt all this you see in the first few months, and even though my team consists of twelve, I keep in touch with them all and find out what they are doing. It is imperative to keep that fire and enthusiasm going. Are they going to meetings, and if not why not? You need to be ahead of the game, every single step of the way. Make sure they know what you are doing too so that you can lead by example.

Be a leader, and pretend (if you don't have all the facts right now) if necessary! Show the way! Or as they say: "Fake it till you make it!"

So what else happened this month? Well I've decided to hit the streets (no not as in red light district) but with my prospecting (that's talking to new people). I went out with some of my buddies and we dressed up to the nines in polished shoes and smart togs and walked bravely down the high street with a huge smile handing out little cards with messages on that basically said "there's a better alternative to a J.O. B." or words to that effect. It takes a lot of courage I can tell you, but if you are having fun it really can pay off. We managed to get about two hundred cards out each in an hour, law of averages says that we should get about five to ten enquiries, Hmm we shall see… I've stuck a few ads in the shop window of post offices and had a few replies and I've started to do stuff on my own without my sponsor. Sometimes I really screw up and I know that I've said too much. I get this silence at the end of the phone that tells me I've gone too far – oops! And then you can never, ever get their confidence back, trust me I've been there, done it. Little said the better really, just get them interested, after all this is a once in lifetime opportunity.

"I've got the most amazing business opportunity that I'd like to share with you – when are you free?"

"I'm out looking for exceptional people to join me in my business and I thought you would be perfect"…

There are so many different ways and they are all so easy to say once I got the confidence and I could cope with people saying no. It doesn't hurt so much when you don't take it personally. And there *will* be people saying no – lots and lots and lots of them because we are sceptical by nature and there's no such thing as a good thing for a lot of folk. There just has to be a catch, doesn't there? Hey how can anything be this good? How do I know? because so many people have said no to me.

I'm getting the hang of this now.

If you spot a really good person and you don't know them, or maybe you've collected a business card a good way to approach them may be along these lines:

"Hi, you don't know me directly, but a colleague of mine gave me your business card – (or I acquired your card from…). The reason for my call is that my company is expanding and we are looking for business professionals to help us in this expansion. So my question is are you open to generating a second income outside of what you are currently doing without compromising your current situation on a part time basis?"

Bit of a mouthful, but sounds good (of course you'll have to read it the first dozen times before it rolls of the tongue)
I've got quite bold of late and sometimes I just say to people:

"I really think you need to look at this opportunity – it's changing my life it could change yours"

"What have you got to lose?"
"Hey if you're too busy who do you know that would like this opportunity to get rich?"

"I know you said this isn't for you, but could you give me the names of 3 or 4 people who you think would like to make some money?/would like this opportunity?"

I'm getting better at this...

I went clay shooting this month, it was the best thing! My husband used to do this stuff, and my son in the States used to sit in the traps and pull the clays all hours of the day and night to earn a few extra bucks in the freezing night air. But anyway here I was with a few girls and we had a go for three hours. We didn't wear all the fancy attire (you know the socks with the tassels etc.) but it was actually really quite good, a bit tricky, especially the overhead shots where you can't see the clay. Actually I did pretty well for a novice, eighteen out of twenty four clays, not bad for a first attempt. Clay shooting is a bit like MLM, especially when you do those over head shots. You get yourself all ready and lined up for it, keep your eye and arm steady and have a feel for when the timing is right, and then you pull the trigger. You can't see the clay at all in the great blue yonder but you know it's coming. You have to have faith in the coach, after all he knows what he is doing. If you listen to the coach and do as he says you can usually hit the target. Sometimes you miss completely, but sometimes you get it spot on – the more times you do it though the better you get it, the better the timing is, and the more times you get lucky! So keep trying! Plus you have to really, really believe the guy when he says "fire" and you can't see a damn thing!

I also went dragon boat racing (excuse me?) What can I say, it's been a long and interesting month! Twenty people in a forty foot canoe on the Thames, quite a challenge I can tell you. I was chief drummer (loved that bit) sat at the front and did the beat, the easy bit you know, we did pretty well actually didn't fall in at all not like some teams. It was teamwork again, we all had to do the same, all had to keep in time and guess what it worked! I was proud of that, all the organisation etc. A sense of achievement always works well for making you feel good.

What a day and it was oh so hot!

Diary of A Network Marketer

What else this month? Oh yes I did a small stint in a tv play because I do all this extra stuff that is quite good fun, except on this day we sat around in a damp bus for eight hours as it was too wet to roll our bit. Still it was fifty quid so you can't complain. Hey I'm a star! Amanda Holden was in it but I didn't get to see her as she was out on location and I was stuck in the bus. I didn't know who she was at the time and then I saw her on telly a few months later and recognised her. Ah well. I prospected the caterers but they were too wrapped up in what they were doing – pennies for old rope but I was having fun anyway.

Isn't life great?
People I signed up : 0 (zip!)
Cheque this month: £121. 72 (oops!)
Product launches 4
Training's loads
Days off none
Drop outs ?
Phone calls not so many probably only 2 a day
Books read : "MLM Nuts & Bolts" (Jan Ruhe), "Fire Up!" (Jan Ruhe), Upline Magazine, "End the struggle and dance with life" (Susan Jeffers)
Tapes: heaps including Randy Gages' "Escape the Rat Race"

Tip of the month: Make sure your team, understand the sense of urgency – it's no good simply waiting for people to call you, you have to get back on to them and quickly! 42 hours or less! Phone them to make sure that they have. Business planning sessions with new distributors need to be done within days of them signing up to keep them excited..

MAY
And Midsummer Night Murders

Hey – here we are again on location! This time with John Nettles and guess what I get a part! I *actually* get a part. All of twenty seconds – blink and you'll miss me hey who cares! I'm famous! I've had *more* than my fifteen seconds of fame. It was so fab, pouring with rain and everyone running around with umbrellas so that I didn't get wet all for one and a half seconds of footage and I was a star and I saw it on telly four months later (taped it of course!) And I adopted a son for the day, but he wasn't like mine thank god – not even close but it was fun. And the lady who shortens my clothes (we can't *all* be 5'10) actually saw me on the telly, what fun all in the blink of an eye as well! I never let an opportunity go by so I was pitching whilst I was there and funnily enough the sound guy had got involved sort of with FLP. It was interesting, but he hadn't been looked after (not many people in his neck of the woods) I've still got his number must give him a ring. Bit of hike Norwich, but what the heck...

Went for my Supervisor lunch this month up at HQ – it was brilliant.

"Do you want to ride in my Mercedes Car....."

I saw a blue metallic SLK and got all fired up – that's me sunshine! Leather trim, CD player the lot and the wind in my hair... Music cranked up to the limit and roaring down the coastal paths of Southern Spain..

Hey! I'm on the way, I just seem to be going along at a snails pace, why aren't things happening quicker? I want it all now! And just why is it that I seem to get my up and go last thing at night – ahh!

Later... Much later..
I'm having a bummer of a week. It's no good, why aren't people doing what they are supposed to do don't they want it badly enough? Get with the programme people! Someone said to me recently "You can't want this for someone else unless they want it" how true! Do you know it is so frustrating when you can see it all – it's right there for all of us for the taking, but many of you don't want it!!! It's like banging your head against a brick wall. (And I don't do *that* very often).

I've been on the phone again calling up those people I know who are working ridiculous hours, in a Job they hate. "Hey look at what I have on offer – it's so wonderful! You can wrap it around whatever you are doing, I won't let you fail," but you know what, they don't want to know, they're afraid they will fail, it's not for them. By now you think you've heard every excuse on the earth. I don't give up though; I give gentle reminders every now and then and let them know the opportunity is still there for when they are ready. I think I might compile a book full of excuses so that when I hear a new one I can write it down.

Oh and some of my team are not doing a *single solitary thing*.

I'm still on a huge learning curve. I'm still trawling though my warm list . (well sort of, I didn't really lie earlier, it was just that I had given up on it and I'm back tackling it again). I've made a really good table, which sets everything out with names, numbers comments etc. It keeps me on track. To date:

I've called: loads of people
Heaps have said no
Heaps have said maybe ..later
Some have said they'll buy the products
Some have said "I'll see how you get on" (ha I'm well ahead of you kiddo!)

Plus I'm getting quite organised. I've got a daily planner because I've got a load of stuff to do and a lousy memory, this way I can sort of keep on track. I've got different files for different things. I make sure my new team members get copies of everything but only step by step you can't give it to them all at once otherwise its overload! Still doing those monthly training's and now we are having "group sizzles" fun meetings when we all get together and share ideas and do a bit of training. *"What do you mean you can't come? Just how serious are you about all of this?"*

Cheque this month: £106.99 (Is there a pattern here? Mmm need to get back into gear!) It seems to be going up and down.
People signed up:2
Product launches one or two (for new distributors)
Books: "Living with Passion" (Peter Hirsch), "Think & Grow Rich" (Napoleon Hill), "17 secrets of the Master Prospectors" (Kalench)

Phone calls A few (not as many as I should be doing)
Drop outs: None

> **Tip of the month: Give credit and never stop praising!** When someone in your group has sponsored someone – make sure you give them tons of praise, let them know just how great they are!

JUNE
& Jonathan...

Yep! It's here again, birthday time! I honestly get quite muddled about how old I am each year because I can never be bothered to keep track, I've been 40 now for the past 4 years, it's quite good actually. My DNA is in regression as I'm taking supplements that are supposed to slow the ageing process – fascinating! At this rate I'll be turning twenty-one again in ten years time! I just love birthdays.. yours mine, anyone's...

I can feel a song coming on..

We went up to the Lake District and had a great weekend walking, except that I'm totally useless going uphill, I just want to be at the top straight away, all the huffing and puffing, but it's worth it for the fab views when you get there! And all that sweat and feeling fit all of three hours and then the taste of cold lager on your lips which helps the downhill track, I'm positively running by the time I get to the bottom! Where's the Heineken!

So June, let's see where am I? I've started to build quite a good group and I've still got a load of people that just buy stuff which is great because it still counts towards the group volume. Case credits and all of that. I'm proud to say that I am now finally getting my head around the marketing plan, just don't ask me to explain it to a group of people. And there are people who I think could possibly be leaders too, people like me, (well, not *quite* like me you understand, I'm a one off) now that's exciting, but actually I really do want people like me because I am so focussed now and on a mission, I do want people who can lead the way and motivate their group.

Later..

I'm having my ten minutes of being miserable. *I am* allowed after all. I mean life is like that isn't it? A week of no shows, no interest and running around after people who quite simply are not really bothered. *And* people telling me they want the business and then not returning phone calls, or worse still saying they will meet you and then not even having the courtesy to let you know they've bottled out. Didn't want them in my business anyway...

Plus whilst I'm on this tack I might as well let you know it's so frustrating! I've been working away and still my cheque is so minimal, but then hey, I'm doing the groundwork, laying the foundations and all this stuff at the beginning will payoff triple fold later. Be patient I hear myself saying, just hang on in, it's all going to happen! And it will, you have to have faith and keep getting people in the team and putting them through training as fast as possible, not next week, this week! Plus I seem to be paying out more than I'm paying in at this moment in time for marketing material etc., etc. HOWEVER and it is a big however I've learnt to realise that I have to invest in my future. Hey if I want a business that turns over in excess of a million I need all the stuff in the world to make it work and so I am telling my new people to hang on in there and invest in training and materials etc, etc, and in time it will pay off. Have a little faith...

Which reminds me somewhat of George Michael and my life long ambition to do a duo (do you know I wrote to him last year and sent him a sample CD and he never wrote back? Tell a lie his record label wrote back to say they couldn't accept anything for him - truthfully I don't know why he hangs out with Geri H.. I would be far more entertaining...)

I'm sure Robert is in despair sometimes - still it makes life interesting..

I used to get stopped by the police all the time in the states for speeding and never got a ticket in ten years but that's another story..

AND I met Michael Jacksons' promo Manager who took a great interest in me, gave me a Pia Zadora tee shirt (that she had given him) (who's Pia Zadora?) and phoned once on his way to the grammys in LA from his limo just to say hi, maybe he thought I had potential...that's another story as well..

The Jonathan day was this Saturday and as usual spectacular, I haven't missed one and I come home revived, inspired, motivated and on such a high I can't imagine ever not going. I rose at the crack of dawn, half comatozed and legged it up on the motorway so that I have a half of a half of a chance of a decent seat, it's always such a mad scramble, a real bun fight for the best seats when the doors open, bit like going to see Paul McCartney in concert really, everyone trying to get in to see the show do or die! But I have to say, yes it's worth it. It's a chance for me to catch up with new friends, listen to truly inspirational messages, see people get up on stage to get their recognition, realise I need to pull my finger out when

I see others doing the impossible and there are usually tears, laughter and I always come away with a warm fuzzy feeling....

So where were we oh yes: People signed up: 1
Cheque: £198.41
People not doing anything still: loads
Product launches: ALOT
Books: "Rich dad, Poor Dad" (Robert Kiyosaki), "Winnie the Pooh on Management & Problem solving," "Questions are the Answers" (Alan Pease)
Tapes: Ageless Body, timeless Mind (Deepak Chopra), Conversations with Jim Rohn

> **Tip of the month: Be active!** Stop putting things off that you said you were going to do today – take action and move your business forward every single day.

JULY
Fun, fantasy & frivolity

Where is the year going? I just can't believe it's July already. If I really pull my finger out I could achieve the next position on the Marketing plan next month which is that of Assistant Manager. It all depends now on everyone doing their little bit and me doing mine, plus one of my team has just gone to Supervisor so I am really so chuffed for them, see it does work! I've got quite a few team members who are going for positions so it's all getting terribly exciting!

It's the ball finally! What ball? My summer ball of course, one that I've organised to raise money for the Bansang Hospital in The Gambia. Don't you just love balls? Black tie and great frocks and lots and lots of wine flowing. Had to get a frock you know but I did very well because purely by chance I saw this drop dead beaded dress in the sale – I need to lose 10 lbs to get into it so I just had to buy it – incentive don't you know... All in a good cause and the first and last (probably) that I will do .. Its been fun, hard work, but fun and in a aid of a great charity. I was sorely tempted to do the network marketing bit, and did refrain (a little) but still clobbered a few people at the bar by which time they were well past sober anyway so that was a waste of time.

And what else? Went for my costume fitting at Angels and Bermans (*the* costumiers of England my dear). When you get into filming you see it just gets so *terribly* exciting. So there I was in awe marching up and down floors and floors of fantastic costumes, from every play and film conceivable (hey even Mel Gibson films - I mean all the costumes for Braveheart and I was standing amidst them all) I was there – I mean there! On the battlefield! Anyway I had to have a frock for this new film Bedazzled with Liz Hurley (yep you read right) and there I was with another lassie stripping off to our bare essentials trying not to look (women do look you know), and me wishing I had the washboard stomach and the legs up to the armpits, but then I've got the lot on top you know so it all evens out in the end. And then lacing up these tight bodices (I could see the fitting girl quite eyeing it all up and making hints about the ample bozoooms and how skimpy the tops were,) and layers and layers of hula hoops the mind boggles and petticoats oh lordy all those petticoats. You know I should have been the next Scarlet O Hara, I did send off my photo when I was living in the States and they were auditioning but they never got back to me – I would have been so good... "Oh Mr. Darcy, Kiss me Mr. Darcy..." They missed their chance. Anyway, I had the greatest costume – indigo satin skirt and low off the shoulder tight fitting top. And they spent hours wrapping my hair and putting in ribbons...

I felt simply *fabulous*...

AND WHAT ABOUT THE NETWORK MARKETING?

Well amongst all this running around having fun I did actually still do some work (marvellous how you can fit it all in). I went out and blatantly told people they needed to come and see the business – didn't put up with anyone who was negative. Just marched on nonchalantly.

How many hours? Well I haven't exactly worked out the number because I'm always far too busy to sit down and do that but I reckon probably about 15 hours a week. Maybe a bit more some weeks, maybe a bit less others. By the way I'm *still* doing my other job just in case you are thinking that I'm not really working.

Plus! I am having so much fun!

Must get organised.. Some weeks I seem to achieve nothing, yet I feel I have worked my socks off. Maybe I need to work a bit smarter..

I'm drawing circles in my sleep...
People signed up: 3
Cheque: £192.28
Retail: £200
Product launches: Yes
Training: Yes lots
People dropped out: can't remember but some not doing much
People going for it: Yes! Lots!
Books: "How to lead a winning group" (David Barber), "Get off to a winning start" (Ditto), "If you can't climb the wall build a door" (Charles Lever)

You might be thinking at this point that in terms of a bonus cheque it's not exactly blow you socks off stuff, however, remember this isn't about getting huge vats of money in the first 6 months, it's about learning and building a business. And don't forget that *In addition* to the monthly bonus cheques your retail can amount to anything from £50 to £500 or more!

> **Tip of the month:** Start calling all those people you rang 6 months ago when you were totally green and didn't know what you were doing them – let them know you are still going strong and having a whale of a time and is the time right for them now to take a look at it all?

AUGUST
Lights, camera, action!

Early August we did the filming in Richmond Park, no glimpse of Liz, but we did mix with Brendon Fraser (who? I didn't know either) (the guy from the movie "The Mummy") it was such fun and a warm day. I had been out gadding the night before with an old girlfriend and had been promptly sick due to too much alcohol. In the early hours and in total darkness I managed to struggle down two flights of stairs, and drank half a glass of Aloe (yes I did take it with me) and for those of you curious to know it did actually help and I didn't have a hangover next day! Got up very early (5 a.m. God help us) to be on set for 6.00 a.m. and I didn't know where the hell I was going. Make up and hair and then stuck in this corset until midnight that night, so going to the ladies was more than a challenge it was an impossibility. What a commotion we caused in Richmond but what fun it was! What a life – movies, men and madness!

And how is the business this month?

Aha, I thought you would ask me that. Just because I am gadding about trying to kick start my career as a legendary movie actress doesn't mean that I'm not doing what I need to be doing. Far from it! I cannot tell you just how fired up I am. Let's see. I'm always talking to people somewhere, somehow about changing their lives, plus I phone John and Jayne almost every day to share what's been going on (or what hasn't) and they don't mind. They are my inspiration, my motivation and my mentors, they lead, I follow all the way…If I need to jump through hoops of fire – heck I'll do it. (Walking on water might be difficult). They're probably sick to death of me by now.

And? Well my other half is just a blessing. He's so great and gives me so much support and can see it all coming together, I can't wait for the time that he can give up his job and do this with me – what a team!

And my son, Lawrence was twenty this month, TWENTY! He's catching me up. I truly can't believe it, I just want the whole world for him and boy am I going to get it!

Diary of A Network Marketer

My daughter Laura is taking driving lessons and it scares me to death that she's going to pass and I'm going to have a whole set of new things to worry about. She's too young to be let loose on the roads for goodness sake! I don't want them to keep growing up I just like it the way it is. But do you know I just love this network marketing so much I'm starting to tell them about how they can get involved, maybe not now but later, it's never too early and it can pave they way to financial freedom for them. I'm so excited about their future.

At the end of the month Sam and I went to a huge country fair. It was one of those crafty dos, lots of quilting, home made jams, candles, and tons of animals, dogs cats rabbits etc. Enormous fun! We took a clipboard, plucked up courage and just asked people 3 questions:

"Did you take time off work to be here today?"
"Would you like to earn an extra £1,000 part time alongside your full time job?"
and
"Can I send you some free info?"

(Can you believe there were folk who really *didn't* want to earn any money? Incredible!) They were lying of course. I nearly died with one lady she was very you know "Oh Dahhling – we have simply acres we just don't need the money my dear" (no but she could have done with a face-lift). We got ten really good leads each within 3 hours. And I bought a really cool bracelet that I just had to have even though I was skint;. I'll pay if back later..

Which leads me to shopping.. Or rather "retail therapy" two very important words in a woman's dictionary.

I love shopping, not the grocery kind where you troll around the supermarket (and I always get the trolley with the ridiculous wheel that goes in the wrong direction), and wasting so much time. I mean how many times do you pick up the same piece of fruit? It goes in the trolley, out again onto the conveyor belt, into a bag, then into the car, then you have to unload, then you have to put it all away, such a waste of time. No, *real* shopping. Saks, Fifth Avenue, Harvey Nicks.. You have to be in the mood to shop, *and* having loads of money helps so I don't do it that often, well hardly at all if the truth be known, but having all the time in the world to just cruise along and ogle at all the fabulous stuff on display can be soul lifting. Retail therapy is not just for us ladies but for *you guys too*, it takes you out of the pits of despair and into another world...

I've been to the designer outlet store a lot this month so much so that they know me quite well by now in Villeroy & Boch. Next time I should give them the business opportunity. Next time I will give them the business opportunity. It's Christmas pressies by the way in case you think I'm spending money on myself (I will later trust me) This is what I'm, going to say: *"You know you've been so great to me over the last couple of months I want to say thank you by offering you the chance to build a fantastic business with me.."*

In time I've got the hang of overcoming objections and now I even talk to complete strangers, but it didn't happen overnight. It required confidence in knowing about the company and the products, and there are many times that I'm still lost for words when people throw stuff at me. If I get a really sticky question I tell people I can't explain in detail about the business because I'm still learning. I just say that there is someone I know who can tell them more, the object is merely to see if they are interested in finding out about a business opportunity, and get them to the next stage: the meeting.

See how much I've learnt already?
It just takes perseverance, persistence and the motivation to get down and keep at it.

This month I made Assistant Manager! How great is that? Do you know I never thought I would get there this quickly but I have, how? Well uh I'm not quite sure except that somebody out there is obviously doing something. Interesting thing, Jayne kept telling me it would happen but I didn't believe her, o ye of little faith, now I believe *everything*. Even if you have lots of people doing a little, products get moved and every little helps so don't dismiss those that put in small orders. I've got people in my team, some don't do diddly squat others are going for gold! I'm getting quite serious now (thank Goodness I can hear Jayne say) because It truly means I am on the way to leadership and all that entails, there's no stopping me now kiddo! Funny how when you get recognition it fires you up to work even harder towards your goals. I've now got 3 people in my group who have made it to first base (supervisor) and they are as happy as can be.

And do you know what? It doesn't matter to me that there are people who've got to where I am in half the time. This is *me, my* business and it doesn't always happen like that - not if like most of us you have a full time job, and a family. What matters is the amount of energy you put into the time you *do* have - and working smart. I know there are some people in my group who seem to put in 20 hours a week and still don't seem to progress, it's about using time effectively. It's about identifying the leaders in the team and working with them. And it's about looking after number one. You.

I was reading a glossy mag this month and found a really fab picture of Pamela Anderson so I cut off her head and kept the body bit and stuck it on my dreamsheet. Dream on baby....

I think one of the most important things when you have new people is to get them up to that first level on the compensation plan as quickly as possible. Why? Well it instils confidence that they can do it. It creates excitement that they now have a team, and that their business is growing, and it proves to them that they can do it, just as you can. Plus once they start duplicating then they start getting cheques - even a cheque for one pound fifty is still a cheque! Alot of people are fearful that they will never get to where they want to be, they see others doing it but can't imagine themselves standing there. It is so essential to sit and plan with them what they will do every day of every week, and to be there for them to cheer them on and motivate when they get down, and boy do they get down! Network Marketing is like a roller coaster ride, one minute you are on a real high because you have found a great prospect (new person) and then you hit rock bottom with a crash because one of your team quits! Ah well such is life, Next!

Diary of A Network Marketer

Product launches: Can't remember, I'm doing them for everyone at the mo.
Cheque: £318.82! Yes!
Dropouts: A few (naturellement)
People signed up: 0 (zip!)
Trainings: Every week
Books read: "The 7 habits of highly successful people" (Steven Covey), "Bread Winner Bread Baker" (Sandy Elsberg), "The Richest Man in Babylon" (George S. Clason)

> **Tip of the month: Build confidence in your group – remind them of their dreams.**

SEPTEMBER
Madeira, Madeira

I'm fed up with all this rain – but it *is* getting warmer. I'm dreaming of that fabulous house right on the ocean near the mountains. Let's go away I said; stuff the overdraft we need a break. Clear out the cobwebs. So off we went. We arrived at Heathrow only to find out that when we went to draw out some money for the trip in the lounge, that we were already well overdrawn and so I had to make an urgent phone call to the bank and plead. Don't worry I heard myself say, things are looking up, this is just all so great, let us hang in and lend us the money! We're going away for two weeks so I want to have some fun and forget about the money until we come back and then we'll worry! All will be good in the end!

Madeira was great, hated the landing bit (not a good flyer and I don't do turbulence). I tried (unsuccessfully) and rather half heartedly, to talk to a rather podgy gentleman sitting next to me about the business, he was an accountant and frankly bored the pants off me (tell me what *exactly* is interesting about accounting?) He wasn't interested.

I've started leaving my business cards in the ladies loos in posh hotels, in fact I leave them in loads of public places, well you never know do you who might just pick them up? Mine are really good though I say so myself, they've got this really fab beach on the front in colour and then some really good words on the back and I got them laminated. What can I say, I'm a stickler for presentation and I really like them. And in case you were wondering, no they weren't that expensive either.

So back to Madeira. We had a great time, lots of sun, lots of romping around in the bedroom (funny how holidays do that) lots of booze and late nights and getting silly and just chilling out. The scenery's great and wonderful places to go in the mountains particularly if you like walking; they have levadas in Madeira, funny little channels of water halfway up the mountains that you can follow for miles.

Madeira really lived up to its reputation for wrinklyville – so I'll maybe go again later. Much later.. We didn't get to Reids hotel but we could see it from our balcony. And we had workmen working right next door building a five star Savoy hotel, which of course they didn't tell us about, so I couldn't wonder around the balcony with very little on, as you do.. We started off with a good room but right on the main road so we had a rotten night and I was fanackerpanned in the morning. I was on a mission to get a different room. Preferably one by the pool over looking the ocean. You know when you feel good about things and if you ask nicely things *do* happen. What is it they say "Manifest your destiny". The next day I asked the concierge sweetly had he got another room? "No madam" was the response in pigeon English. Undeterred I went back downstairs 20 minutes later on a different tack and turning on all the worldly charm I could muster, you know the whole nine yards.

Despite the fact that the whole hotel was booked we ended up with the best room over looking the pool away from the road that slept six instead of two, you see being nice to people works wonders. Oh and we hit a bus on a mountain road. Couldn't avoid it really as it was on our side and we demolished the left wing. Halfway up the blooming mountain and no we had decided *not* to take out the extra cover this time round (hey we never have an accident), so we ended up having to fork out three hundred pounds for damages. C'est la vie..

I don't know about you but I really love going away, it seems that we get back some of what we had. Kind of re-live our youth so to speak. With the stress in our lives we never seem to do the stuff we used to, never have the fun, or if we do it's few and far between. Life just isn't the same as when you are in your twenties, carefree and haven't yet got entrenched in the pitfalls of the rat race. Somehow, when you go away, even if its only for a few days, you capture some of that freedom, isn't it wonderful! You mess around, stay up all hours, get silly, do lots and lots, get that all over sun kissed glow, and you feel great because you look great And then a week later you come back down to earth with a jolt and carry on again for another year. How we long for our time out, how precious it all is and how wonderful. Well that's all going to change because guess what? I'm going to have more time to do more, more time to travel and see the world. More time for life.

What about the business? I was concerned about going away for two weeks in fact I panicked because I really didn't want to leave my team on its own, what could happen? It could all fall apart! But do you know when I got back my cheque had almost doubled! And whilst I was away, yes I still took some of my stuff with me and I still asked for business, sold all the products I had taken with me (all two tubes of gelly). You've just got to ask.

Oh and I got the Villeroy & Boch girl on this month yipeee! She knows thousands and thousands of people - I'll be rich! Ahhh!
Persistence has paid off!

RESIDUAL INCOME AND ALL THAT JAZZ..

Network marketing brings you the freedom to have time out. Hey, I know I'm still a novice but I do understand how it works. I haven't got to that bit yet when you can just swan off for a few months and not worry, but I do meet so many people who *have* reached that point. All good things come to those that wait. (Patiently or otherwise). So how does that happen I hear you ask? You work hard at getting yourself up and running and building a great business and then residual income kicks in. Residual what? Well, this is what is so fantastic about Network Marketing; you start a duplication process. You teach people what you have been taught and get them to do the same. Eventually you end up with tons of people all who have been brought into your group by other people in your group and it just grows and grows. It eventually reaches a point where there are so many people that you have what's called residual income: income that just keeps on coming (bit like the energiser bunny!) now how cool is that?

Oh boy and I've just got to tell you about one of my prospects. Sorry I'm off on a whim again. This is how ludicrous it gets sometimes and to what lengths you go to! I had this chap who followed me for half an hour on the motorway in speeds of over ninety trying to get my phone number (I have "*Trainee millionaires wanted*" written all over my BM) and the long and short of it all was that I got him interested in the business.

Great! I can hear you saying. Well let me tell you this guy was the biggest waste of space. I legged it all the way to London (about an hour and a half from me) with my sponsor who incidentally is a big cheese in my eyes, and this chap had the audacity to take a phone call from his friend for twenty *minutes* no less in his fluffy beaver slippers *Whilst we were sitting there waiting,* I mean how rude can you be? I made a mental note right there and then that it was the chops for him, didn't want him, nah, don't need people like that thank you. He then proceeded to say he wanted a yacht that was going to cost him at least £250,000, there as he sat in his semi and his fluffy slippers, and with that attitude? Not a chance sunshine, keep dreaming!

This is a *great* business.

Cheque: £414.26! (It's really on its way up)
Retail: £250
Product launches: lost track but about one a week for team members
Training's Yes of course
Meetings Naturally
Drop outs None
Books: "The Basics" (Don Failla), "Just what is Network Marketing?" "The Art of Happiness" (HH Dalai Lama)
Signed up: 3

> **Tip of the month:** Seek out the leaders and work with them don't waste time with people who don't bother attending meetings or training's, they aren't serious business builders..

OCTOBER
"Trainee Millionaires Wanted"

I got a speeding ticket today.
It was one of those days. There I was rushing to see a customer all raring to go, all cylinders firing (as you do!) Whoosh, round the corner straight into the eye of a laser gun and two very nice policemen. Well there's not a lot you can do really is there? I smiled somewhat cheesily, after all they were out to get someone that day, it just happened to be me typically. Let's face it, blazing down the trails has to be frowned on. Anyway I decided that it wasn't worth all the fresh air arguing so when this nice policeman, Frank his name was, had finished telling me I was going to have points on my licence (poo) he also saw the signwriting on my car. "Trainee Millionaires wanted". He grinned and asked was that me? I looked around, bit of a daft question I wanted to say but instead I said "Of course it's me – well it will be soon". And then not wishing to waste an opportunity I asked him if he wanted to earn some extra income, a fabulous opportunity, a great lifestyle. He smiled and yes he would, so we swapped cards. You see there's something around every corner waiting for you. Even if it is a laser gun! Always turn things around into your favour, it makes the day so much brighter! Wish it was always this easy.

I'm on a mission. I know they're out there, all those people that want to win the lottery, or otherwise. I mean who wouldn't want to be a Trainee Millionaire for goodness sake? I love my car, it's got all this cool writing all over it and always brings a smile whenever I'm out and about. I don't care if it's a bit naff – it works! I can't say they are all queuing up to talk to me exactly but it is a talking point. I think people are more than a bit sceptical about blatant advertising . I wonder if I put an ad in the paper that said "Trainee millionaires wanted" whether I'd get any phone calls…Anyway back to the car - next time I'm going to have glow in the dark signwriting so you'll see me coming a mile away! It's going to say "Millionaire in training follow me"… or words to that effect..

I'm starting slowly but surely to get rid of the clutter. A cluttered house is a cluttered mind. So, what did I do? Well, I finally sold the ball and claw dining room table, the old leather desk and the black leather suite that didn't go with anything and that we were hanging on to. I've decided I'm going to go through each room throughout the house and really be ruthless, (again), all that junk sitting in drawers that we haven't touched or looked at in the last three years. It's all going to Bosnia or Oxfam or breast cancer or the homeless. I can't bear to think of all the money that we've wasted over the years on useless stuff...

And I've taken a good hard look at where my business is going. Or isn't more to the point. I've come to the sudden realisation (well that's not quite true Jayne has been telling me for months) that I need to get out and sponsor more and stop running around after my team, like a mother goose. It's interesting how things have cooled down somewhat, and when I look at my activity I'm beginning to realise that I *am* concentrating far too much on two legs of the business and not enough on sponsoring and that's what is going to make the cheque grow. So! Another learning curve and now I am going to focus on getting at least five more new team members front line to me!

Network Marketing is about helping others. People out there in this world have stopped dreaming. Remember when we were children and dreams were everything? All things were possible then. We were going to be astronoughts, actresses, rock stars, Now we are older we are not allowed to follow our dreams, well most of us anyway. So isn't it great to be able to say to people, "hey you can still have the things in life you want if you just let me show you". It doesn't matter if you are new in the business; there are tons of people around who have been in a lot longer who can help you help them.

Do you believe in fairies?

Diary of A Network Marketer

People signed up: 4
People dropped out: none that I know of
Cheque: £535.71!
Retail: £200
Training Yes, always
Books read: "Optimum Nutrition" (Patrick Holford), "The New Professionals" (King & Robinson)
Tapes: Randy Gage's collection on "How to build a $100,000 money making machine" (Brilliant!)

> **Tip of the month: Revise your goals constantly and reward yourself when you achieve them. Set small goals as well as big ones.**

NOVEMBER
Of champagne and charlatans

The fall colours are somewhat upon us, but not like the fall in New Jersey which has the most spectacular colours: burnt umber, deep red, brilliant yellows and every shade of brown, sienna, orange you can think of. We used to drive up to the Delaware Gap to see the fall. I miss the fall in New Jersey. But hey! Here we are in sunny old England and the autumn in special here too, just too much rain! It really doesn't seem to have ceased these last few weeks, just coming and coming. England is sinking, floods everywhere soon there'll be just one small island right on top. Will it ever stop raining? Fall arrived late this year. I think the weather got slightly confused and we are enjoying an Indian summer. I had one of those (ahh) moments today driving home. It was late afternoon. Cold (bitterly) but bright and gloriously sunny. Blue skies and the sunshine catching the vividness of the leaves in all their brilliant colours. However the leaves are falling now rapidly and the nights are drawing in quickly. I awake to mornings of crisp white frost, and catch my breath in the morning air.

I can't contain myself this month; I'm going for Manager on our marketing plan, I love all this recognition stuff!! Whoopee it's all coming together. And it's all there all within my reach. The team is all doing OK in fact they are doing *more* than ok they are doing just great, and yes there are people who are really doing not a lot except star gazing, but hey that's ok because we've got more people on board who I really think are going to be so great! You know my philosophy this month is just get lots and lots and lots of people doing a little. You still need to duplicate because that's what's going to get you into the millionaires club, but for now lay down the foundations. Jayne told me a really good story. She said: Be patient. Remember when you had your house built? There was this big hole in the ground and every day for weeks and weeks and months and months it remained a big hole, but stuff was going on down there even though you couldn't – well occasionally you'd poke your head down and see that there was stuff going on, quite a lot actually! Well, much much later the bricks were laid and then suddenly this beautiful house appeared, you'd drive by and there it was! That's what network marketing is all about, lots of foundation work, working your whatsists off and not seeing the results until everything is firm and stable.

Diary of A Network Marketer

Someone responded to one of my post office ads three months ago and it has been a bit of a slog getting them on board but I did persevere because I just felt that they would be right for the business. It has paid off now and what a superstar I have in my team, it's really exciting when you get someone who goes all out for it like you, in fact if I could duplicate myself, make lots of little Phillys I would be laughing! Anyway in this first month Michael and his wife Sally have just astounded me, gone out and already got two people on board, plus they have managed to retail huge amount of product, so much so, that in five weeks they have got to the first level of the marketing plan wow! That's going some. I am overjoyed for them because they feel so great at their achievement. See! It *can* be done if there's the determination!   And? I went to hear a truly great inspirational speaker this month. Now I've heard that there are these great mentors out there, people who give so much and from whom you can learn volumes, and let me tell you there can be no other great mentor that I aspire to than my own sponsors, but I had the privilege of meeting Jan Ruhe this month, what an incredible person, what an inspiration! There are many great leaders in Network Marketing, people who have achieved such amazing things through their own determination, that to miss them sharing on how they did it would be like cutting off your leg (or some other similar analogy!)
So if you hear that someone great in Network marketing is coming to your country, beg, steal or borrow so that you can get there, it will be worth its weight in gold! I am so fired up! From that *one* day my thought process turned a hundred and eighty degrees, and my mind was full of new directions and processes. It went completely into overload and I couldn't sleep for weeks, plus everything now seems so much clearer.

Today it is wet and cold oh yes and foggy. I called into Head office to see how I am getting on to getting to Manager – still a long way off and only ten days to go. It will happen. I have said so.

And Charlie our golden retriever has been leaving my underwear all over the house again.

I came home to find a pair of knickers on the stairs, a pair of tights in the hallway and a bra in the kitchen! Thank goodness I wasn't bringing Mel Gibson home.

He just loves his job, you name it he will fetch it and if you can't find it? Well you probably will eventually. I found the remote control in the backgarden a few weeks ago and well he just has this fetish for my undies particularly when we have guests over....

I digress..

This is just a short story to say that many of your days will be wasted so do try and find out as much info as possible before you make your journey. One of my team had a really hot prospect this week so we decided to go and pay him a visit. Off we went Tony and I, all the way to the ends of the earth to present our fabulous opportunity. We arrived on this wet day to a portakabin which didn't even have had enough room to swing a cat. Not only was it was hard work it was incredibly depressing and I couldn't wait to leave. Well this chap had his own business, he was into the bouncy castle thing, and Tony had assured me he had primed him. He was ready and waiting. I'll say. The office was different to say the least four people crammed into a room 6 x 4 with three desks, four chairs, two computers and tons of stuff. It was claustrophobic, Tony left after two minutes to get some fresh air before he passed out. We hung around for half an hour whilst Dan finished his telephone conversation and then decided due to lack of space that we would find a local pub where we could spread out our wares.

There were six of us in total, three young girls, and two fellas plus me (that makes six). One was quite happy with what he was doing but wanted to listen anyway, and two young wee things who looked quite blankly ahead most of the time showing no interest at all. And Joe Blo? Sometimes you can just tell when you meet someone that they are not right for the opportunity. Right from the beginning the body language said it all, and well, this guy he really didn't like me, didn't like the fact that there was this female who was going to make it and he wasn't. Sat with his arms folded the entire time and hunched up in the chair. Funny thing was he kept contradicting himself, one minute said he had loads of money., next he couldn't pay the bills. Work that one out. The others really looked on rather clueless, still, I must say I did an excellent presentation. When I asked him if he was interested he said no (quite adamantly I hasten to add).

"What is it that I haven't said that you need to know?" I enquired.

"you're not earning enough money – I'm earning more than that now!"

Well, I suppose I could have sat and made a point but to be honest it would have fallen on stony ground and anyway I decided he wasn't worth the time of day, I didn't want him in my team and it was time to move on. He had missed the point entirely. It was not for him. I told Tony to go back in a year in his snazzy car and let him know what he was missing. He was disappointed and angry that we had wasted time. But actually we hadn't. It had been a learning curve, and at the end of the day one of the girls showed an interest that could well develop into something.

Remember: some will, some wont, so what – Next!

My world is changing hour by hour, day by day, month by month.

And you know what? I can see now how some things go together. You see there is so much to learn and it's not until you get to the end of this first year that all the pieces slowly start to fit together. Piece by piece.. I'm never going to lose sight of my dreams, not ever going to give up.

Monday:
I spent all day preparing for a charity day at my house. In total I had put out four hundred flyers throughout the village, it was a hard slog but I knew it would be worth it. I woke up in the night excited about the day ahead. After weeks of planning the day had arrived. The house was spotless, all the products laid out and it all looked really quite nice. I lit some candles, turned on some classical and waited. And waited. Well, throughout the day only five people turned up, five
out of all the flyers we had put out and all the phone calls. I was determined not to get down, it could have been worse, nobody could have shown up, and they were all in all five nice people, and you know what? They were 5 more clients that I didn't have previously. I suppose what made the day really worthwhile was that pretty much all of the team turned up in support, that's teamwork for you! So to me it was worth it all. So what if not many people could be bothered to come? I realised that I had a strong group, who were all pulling together. How marvellous!

This month Andy brought another great person into my team and they are really going for it, so much so that they have done far more than I have in their first month than I had done in my third! It's wonderful when you have key people who want to really work hard for what they want, and you can see them pulling all the stops out.

I'm panicking with only two days left to go and I still haven't reached my target to manager.

Wednesday….. HIGH AND FLYING!

I've opened the champagne (It's 9.30 in the morning for goodness sake!) and I'm sharing it with one of my team who's made it to Assistant Manager! And as for me well I'm there, it's just a question of adding it all up now, but I know I've done it, there's some apprehension still in the air, but it's in the bag and I cannot tell you what a wonderful feeling it is to have achieved that first goal! This is the bestest thing I have ever done. Why didn't I find this earlier? Plus I had a great meeting last night, lots of nice people saying nice things which isn't always the case. I was on form dare I say it, and it's really all coming together.

People signed up: - 0 (zip!)
Cheque this month lots more
People in the group can't remember
Product launches yes
Dropouts don't know
Trainings: Of course
Phone calls Quite a few but not as many as I should
Books read: "True Leadership" (Jan Ruhe & Art Burleigh) (Fabulous) "How to build a Multi-level Marketing Machine" (Randy Gage) Brilliant book, "The Miracle of Intention" (Pat Davies) Fantastic read!

> **Tip of the month: Find a balance in what you are doing - plan your activity every single day.**

DECEMBER
Snow, Santa Clause and seeing the light..

Today is the first day of December and I have reached the dizzy heights of Manager. So I've made it almost to the end of this first year. If I told you that this year has gone so quickly I am sure you can imagine. I almost feel as though I haven't stopped to catch breath. But I have. I am doing about twenty hours a week now through my own choice, some weeks I do less, some weeks more, but still part time. And yes, I still waste lots of time doing things that are utterly useless!

Oh and the Villeroy & Boch girl dropped out of the business - why? She was too busy with V & B and although she had an incredible need, just loved her job so much she couldn't see the wood for the trees.. Oh Well. Silly me, I didn't get her contact list off her.

It has been an incredible year, lots to learn but such fun. I have made a mountain of friends, and my vocabulary has extended to uplines, downlines, MLM, front loading back loading etc. etc. All totally weird. I've gone back to school in terms of training, reading and learning, and have duplicated my brain cells, which were deteriorating.

This month I launched into speaker training. Decided I was big enough and brave enough to have a go. And it was great. It took me way of my comfort zone, but I still enjoyed it. I have developed as a person, expanded my repertoire, and become more knowledgeable. The greatest thing though above all else, is that there are people in my group who look to me as a leader, to show them the way, and boy does that make me feel special (but somewhat scary).
And I'm more patient.

And if I can help as many of them as possible make it to their goals, well I shall be one very happy bunny.

On the fridge I have stuck my goals for the next five years. I want to be a diamond manager earning at least twenty five thousand a month. I've mapped out what I need to do, how many people I need to talk to each day, how many I need to sponsor and how many managers I need. Piece of cake!

CHRISTMAS & WINNIE THE POOH…

Well Christmas is less than two weeks away and it is pouring with rain yet again. I'm so excited, I am going to get my Christmas tree tomorrow, scramble into the loft and dig out all the decorations, such a great time of year! Where's the snow, heck it needs to snow for Christmas!
We've had a spell of bad luck this past month (well not really bad luck just a run of things going wrong.) Robert got his car broken into (what a pain), then the Firebird broke down on the way home from work so we had to call out the relay at great expense, plus the bank keeps sending me letters, but you know what? Every day is a step closer to our dreams, life is good, life is wonderful and I am just so lucky to have all the things that matter: A great husband, fabulous kids, my family close by, a nice home, health, wealth and happiness! And the most amazing future ahead!

Robert and I went to the Jonathan this month, I've only missed one the entire year, it was lovely to get on the podium with everyone else getting their recognition, and I'm proud of my achievement! What else was really special was that Robert came up with me too, he is so excited about the business and wants to come on board and join in, so our future together is looking more solid than ever. I value his input and support, we shall be a great team! It made me realise as I stood there, a sea of faces before me in the darkness, and my heart thumping and going like an express train, that I had a real sense of togetherness – not just with FLP, but with everyone in our team who had helped us achieve. Without them we simply would not have been there, and sometimes it's so hard to put that into words.

Do you know I saw not one but three shooting stars tonight! I was on my way home from seeing my father singing in The Messiah (gosh it was brilliant). It was a perfect night. Clear skies, full moon (he was positively smiling at me tonight), and then it happened. At first I thought I was imagining it, a falling star, brightly in the sky just for a moment. Moments later another, and then another, I had to pull over before I ended up in the hedge. It was dark and peaceful and I was just so wrapped up in it all that I wanted to share it with someone. I couldn't get through on the home phone (probably on the Internet again) so I phoned the local radio station and had fifteen minutes telling the local DJ about this phenomena.

It's Christmastime and for the first time in years it actually feels Christmassy. I'm sitting by the fire all warm and toasty, it's cold and wet outside, no sign of snow but I live in hope. A glass of ice cold sherry tingles on my lips and I snuggle up to watch yet again "A Christmas story". Hope I get Tigger the movie this year in my stocking because that's on my list to Father Christmas. Winnie the Pooh is just my favourite of all time.

People signed up: 1
Training's: Tons
Books read Loads
People dropped out: Can't remember as it loses significance

Cheque: £1750! Duplication has definitely begun!

> **Tip of the month: Be happy. Be positive. Generate a warm fuzzy feeling where ever you go and see how people will want to find out more about what you do. Smile at everyone you meet and pay a compliment to anyone you bump into…**

So total figures for the year: Well I signed up twenty-two which I'm pretty proud of, so I've set my goal for next year to be fifty (positive thinking here) that's one a week (well almost).

What a great year it has been, and what achievements we have seen. Together, moving all the goalposts yet again to make our dreams closer. The world looks definitely a better place...

LEARNING CURVES AND BITING THE BULLET

I'm still so new at all of this but I have learnt some important lessons over the last year.
One of the greatest things, the most important perhaps of all, is not to waste time on people who didn't want the business opportunity.

Ha! Easier said than done my friend! It's somewhat of a chicken and the egg situation because when you are new how can you possibly tell who is right for it and who isn't? Plus let's face it we want anyone and everyone at the beginning right? Well yes and no.   Let me help you out a little.

When you start all fired up and raring to go, what's the first thing we all do? Right! We rush out and try and get as many people signed up as possible because we are so desperate! However take a few words of caution from someone who has found out the hard way. There are three kinds of people out there:

1. *The first kind* you talk to say no and mean no, but we still try and persuade them they need the business.

2. *The second kind* show an interest but the time really isn't ready for them right now, we may succeed in signing them up but it's like dragging a horse to water that doesn't want to drink, they don't go to the training and they are always too busy to put time into their business. Reality is the timing isn't right for them.

3. *The third kind* are the ones that sit up and are excited. They tell you there and then they want it – they have energy in their voice and are ready to go. Fantastic!

At first we are all of us blinkered and we spend an enormous amount of time, energy, money and effort into getting types one and two fired up. Taking them to training etc and wanting the business for them more than they want it themselves. Fact.

Save yourself some time..
Looking back I can see how much time I have wasted with people and when I think back to the first meeting I had with them, I can now see they simply weren't ready or weren't interested. In the long run you will waste a lot of effort. Hey that's going to happen whatever I say, it's just that I'm trying to cut it down for you. So what do you do? Well, when you talk to people about the business take a step back and ask yourself:

Is this person really interested?
Are they ready – now?
Do they want it?
How badly do they want it?
Are they excited about the prospect?
Do they have dreams?
Do they need financial security and will they be prepared to go all out for it?

If they seem casual, laid back, unenthusiastic, need time to think about it, don't know, maybe, perhaps, very busy, or simply don't need or want the opportunity then let them go! However painful it may be and however much you may think they need it, let them go. Long term: it will save you lots of money. Plus you will find people out there who genuinely DO want the business opportunity and will give you one hundred and fifty percent!

At the very beginning it's tough, no two ways about it. You win some, you lose some and you get extremely frustrated because Network marketing is so great you think everybody needs it. Reality is that not every one does. Some people genuinely *are* happy, *do* have enough money, *don't* want to work from home. Each to their own.

It's a Numbers business...
Bottom line... despite everyone telling me, and me unbelieving, the penny has finally dropped. It's a fact (another one):

The more people you talk to, the more likely someone is to join your business.

One in ten will take it a step further (which means you have to go through nine "No's".

Out of 5 people who join your business:

1 will do absolutely nothing
3 Will do a little
And one will be a Superstar (John Curtis)

So it's kind of like throwing mud at the wall - some of it will stick.

Many will cop out along the way, even those that seem enthusiastic, and some will even start to build a small business before they fall by the wayside. That's the tough side of network marketing: finding good people who understand what it's all about.

It takes a certain kind of individual to go the whole way, but you know what? They are out there, you just have to be persistent and determined and you will find them...

A GIFT

Offering people Network Marketing with Forever Living is akin to offering a very special gift, which of course it is, the best gift of all: Freedom to choose...

Whenever I speak to people about our business I imagine I am giving them a box full of all the wonderful things they want, all wrapped up with a huge gold bow with streams of ribbons hanging down. Inside when they take a peek, they can glimpse at all the things life can offer them, but in particular all those things that they have dreamed about that they thought would never come to light...
And you know what? I've gone back to my old original warm list, the one I started with way back when. Now I've been doing the business a year I know what I'm doing (More or less), still a long way to go but well on my way. Now I'm calling up those people who said "Let me see how you get on" and telling them big time that they are missing out on one heck of an opportunity.

As a person I have grown more confident, I'm bolder, more assertive, I still haven't lost the gentle touch but I see the world through pink coloured lenses now. I'm wiser dare I say it, and passionate about life. I've realised that everything is there for the taking, you just need to reach for it. I've realised that we are all winners, if we choose to be. I've seen that this business can help each and every one of us whatever it is that we seek. I can see that it brings happiness and choices, freedom and a lifestyle most can only wish on a star for.

How great it is to have such a wonderful chance at making all things possible not just for ourselves but for others too.

I'm so looking forward to helping my team reach their goals too, all of a sudden other peoples lives *do* become your business and become important to you. How wonderful to be able to change someone's life so dramatically. How great to be a part of that equation.

And at the end of the day I have stumbled across what has to be the best company in the world. A company that cares, shares and offers a lifetime of opportunities and friendships. How blessed I am to have found this now. However, like all things in life, it isn't all roses and champagne. It's frustrating and difficult, and it can drive you to sheer desperation and tears. But it's worth it for all that it can bring.

AND FINALLY...(WELL ALMOST)

It's hard to get serious about Network marketing when your working business day perhaps is spent socialising in a café downtown talking about the incredible benefits this industry has to offer. But get serious you must, for perhaps the biggest downfall of would be aspiring network marketers is that the whole concept is so simple that when the hard times come (and come they undoubtedly will) - when every character you meet that week eyes you suspiciously and is convinced you are losing your marbles and doing some dastardly deal, you lose sight of your goals, and everything falls apart. But for those that stay focussed - that's the key. Come the time when you can see Network Marketing in all its colours and for what it truly is, to accept the lows along with the highs with a shrug, that's when it gets into your blood.

Let's look at some of the things that were obstacles this first year:

OK SO YOU HAVE TO MAKE A FEW PHONE CALLS:

Facing the phone: (Do you want to change your life today, tomorrow or never?)

This is one of the biggest fears that we all of us, you, me and the rest of the world, have to overcome, it's just simply awful if you are one of those people who is lousy on the phone. However, there are ways to do it to make life a lot easier, let me show you how.

Making that call. Having a glass of wine helps a lot if you are in panic mode but if you don't drink then just go for it kiddo! Just don't get plastered otherwise you'll be spouting off forever about all sorts of rubbish. MINDSET: You have to remember time and time again that this is a numbers game (all right in theory, not in practice when you are desperate to get people signed up). But it IS a numbers game, I've proved it, eventually you do find someone who really wants to change their lifestyle.

And yes it does mean trawling through loads of people but guess what? It will happen so long as you do it all the right way! So *what's* the right way:

Rule #1: Keep it short and to the point. You really *don't* need to give them the whole life history of Southfork Ranch and the bees buzzing happily in the Sonoran Desert.

Have a few notes on what you might say and always have your get out clause *"Love to tell you more but I've got to dash out and take the dog to the psychiatrist"* or whatever then you can make your phone call sweet, short and to the point.

And yes it does help to have some idea of what you are going to say before you pick up the phone. Maybe they have a HOT button. What's a hot button? Well it can be something they are either really good at *("Hey you are so good with people, you have such a great personality"* or it can be a real need that gets them excited: *"you know that detached house you always wanted at… well there may be a way for you to get it"*)

Rule #2: Don't argue with people - if they are negative just move on to the next person.

Rule #3: Have some idea of how you can overcome the common objections:

Rule #4: Remember, you are only the messenger

Things people say:

- I'm too busy
- *Most of us are with the busy lifestyles we have but that's what is so great about this opportunity it takes so little time.*
- *This will enable you to have so much free time to do what you want.*
- Sounds too good to be true
- *It is too good to be true! That's why I want to share it with you*
- must be pyramid selling
- *Pyramid selling is illegal. Network Marketing is fast becoming recognised by huge companies such as Microsoft, Dell and Amazon as a means to reach people quickly and effectively.*
- What's the catch?
- *Why does there have to be a catch?*
- You do it first and I'll see what happens to you
- *Why wait? I'm only just starting out – you too can build a business today, alongside me!*
- How much does it cost?
- *It costs nothing to register, but serious business builders obviously try some of the products to see if they like them*
- I knew someone who did that and lost a lot of money
- *Years ago some people did lose money with pyramid selling. This is something quite different and many thousands of people are reaping the rewards of Network Marketing.*
- It's not for me
- *How do you know it's not for you, I haven't told you anything yet!*

Diary of A Network Marketer

- I can't sell
- *There is very little retail involved.*
- I don't want to sell blah, blah, blah, you know you've heard it (or you will soon trust me)

Bottom line: People are afraid of what they don't know PARTICULARLY IF THEY CAN MAKE A TON OF MONEY!

Well, here are a few more key phrases that may get you out of a sticky mess:

"You know I'd love to tell you more and I'm not being evasive but I'm really new at the business and still learning – However I don't want you to miss out on this great opportunity so why don't we get together with the person that got me on board and they can answer all of your questions. When are you free, tomorrow or Thursday?"

"I'm going to give you so much support there's no way you will fail if you're with me"

"Would you like to start making some money soon, how about next week?"

"Has anything I've said made sense? When can we get together tomorrow or Thursday?"

"Pyramid selling's illegal – do you really think I'd get involved with something like that?"

"This is an honest, ethical and tremendously exciting business!"

ON PLANNING AND HOW DOES IT ALL WORK?:

This took me a while to really sink in but good planning is essential. If you want a really successful business you simply have to plan your activity and your teams activity every month *at the beginning of the month.*

Get yourself a wipey board (a good one otherwise you'll regret it and you'll never be able to rub out) and draw circles of you and who is in your team. Circles are so important in this business. If you can demonstrate growth in this way it just makes sense! I just love circles!

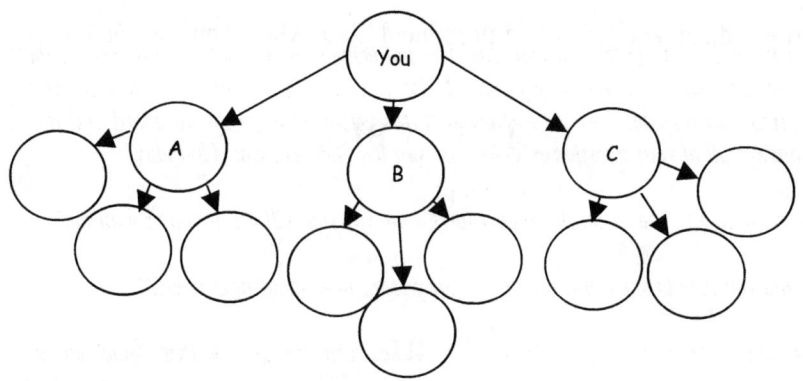

So here's you and you go out and find 3 people
With those 3 people you sit down with them, and ask them who they know who would be interested in the business opportunity. Those 3 know 3 more people giving you 12 altogether in your team but you only found 3.

Look at it another way (the bigger picture) Say you find 5 good people over a period of time and it does take a while, so be prepared to wait!

You 5	=	5
Those 5 find 5	=	25
Those 25 find 5	=	125
Those 125 find 5	=	625
Those 625 find 5	=	3,125
Total in group:	=	3,905

Can you see how duplication has gone crazy? And you still only found *5* not *3,905!* Let me ask you this: who *cannot* get excited about this opportunity? Bottom line it doesn't really happen like this in real life, some wont find any – some will only find one or two, and then someone may find 5 or 6 but it will eventually happen.

So back to the wipey board: draw out your circles, to start with they will look a little lonely, but don't worry they will fill up over time! Work out what people will do this month in terms of sponsoring somebody or having a product evening.

Write it down and put it in a prominent place where you can see it every day.

THINK BIG.

DREAMSHEET – SO WHAT DO YOU WANT, DO YOU *REALLY* REALLY WANT?

I should have been the next Spice Girl I would have been Sexy Spice…(yeah right..)
Goals and dreams are the *essence* of Network marketing. Without your dreams you will never achieve what you want from life. Set your goals and dates and live them daily, visualise them and teach your group to do the same.

So what *do* you really really want? If you want that luxury car go to the dealership, find it, choose the colour and all the accessories (so you want a CD drive, how about a sunroof? Leather interior? What colour? personalised plates?) Take a photo of you sitting in it, better still take it out for a test drive. Stick these pictures on a sheet where you can see it every day. What do your kids want? Maybe a trip to Disney? Go to the travel agent, get the brochures, pick a date and work towards it, then when you are out late they will understand you are doing this for them too. Get them involved, how about your spouse? My husband wants a Harley we've go that stuck on the wall. (Not the Harley, just the photo..) Take pictures as you get recognition at events, take pictures of your team, take copies of all your cheques.

Remember this is *your* company, your very own, however big it becomes it's still your baby. Want to go International, hey, that's no problem if you have the determination. Why not go world wide?

Want to be a great speaker? Start now. Go to the training's, Build up your confidence, heck it doesn't matter if you mess up in front of your friends, remember we are all in the same boat.

You see I've already developed an attitude, nothing's going to stop me and my confidence is really rocketing!

On Attitude:

Attitude is Key. Attitude is success. Want to have a great business? Well whatever comes out of your mouth will determine your future. Think before you speak (even if you are excited). Be positive in your words and actions. If you mess up it's no big deal so long as you let people know you screwed up. So what if you don't know what you are talking about initially? Have at least some of the facts and don't forget: people buy *you*, not the product, not the company, they look at you and your belief and your positive action and <u>then</u> they take a look at the rest.

- Be persistent but not pushy.

- Don't give up on people – let them know there is always a door open if they change their mind.

- Opportunities are around every corner we just don't choose to take them.

- Let people know that you are going to make it with or without them, but that you were rather with them.

- Keep your family posted as to what you are doing and why, let them know you are doing this for them too, try and work to your goals together.

- Hang out with those that are successful, the leaders and achievers. Ask questions, be hungry to learn. Do as they do, that's what I'm doing, heck if they did it and got it right it has to be a little easier for me doesn't it?

WHAT DO YOU DO WHEN YOUR WARM MARKET RUNS OUT?

At some point in time your warm market inevitably runs out. So what do you do? Well you start to tackle the cold market, you know the rest of the world (and by the way you will never, ever run out of prospects no matter what anyone says).

Start to advertise. I got good results advertising in my local post office and corner shop. I also ran small ads in the local free papers and parish news. The message must be different, dynamic, and create curiosity.

Advertising in papers can be costly so do your homework first. Leaflet drops in village halls is inexpensive, find out when toddler group, brownies or scout meetings are held, or maybe even rotary clubs. Anywhere where they have weekly or monthly meetings. You can maybe do a presentation evening at a social club, sports club, health club, hospital or whatever. Be smart with your advertising and make sure that you are prepared for when the phone calls come in. Have a professional answering message and always respond to phone enquiries within twenty-four hours.

And by the way, your cold market soon becomes your warm market. How? Well every time you meet someone new, let's say you go into your local car dealership and you meet the salesman. First time you don't know him, but the next time you go in he is a familiar face, so now you have built a mini relationship and he no longer is your cold market - make sense?

ON BUILDING RELATIONSHIPS

Pay attention here my friends I do believe the key to recruiting is by building terrific relationships with people. And once they are on board by having empathy with them and creating a bond of friendship. After all teamwork is teamwork and works much better if you are with people that you like and trust. So have empathy with everyone.

When I meet people for the first time I now take time out now to find out as much as I can about them. (I didn't when I started, I was desperate to tell them absolutely everything about the company, the products, the opportunity and how they could get rich). Ask lots of questions about their family, job, their values, what they enjoy. I *truly believe* that this is the essence of creating interest. So often we spend so much time getting carried away talking about the business that we don't stop and listen to what people are saying. If you express genuine interest in someone and find out what they want from life you will have a far better success rate with your prospects. I've learnt that if I spend most of the time asking them questions, they are so much more open and relaxed and more willing to listen to the opportunity.
Understand their feelings, situation and what makes them excited. It will get you a long way.

NETWORKING: Buzzword of the new Millennium?

Networking is fast becoming the buzzword of the new millennium and you will come across many people on your travels that are involved in some network marketing company or other, even some that you know! However, you must also be aware that many people will have tried some and failed. They will be the first ones to tell you it won't work because it didn't work for them. In Forever Living they have all their ducks in a row and everyone benefits right from the beginning. It's a company that teaches and trains you to be the best you can be. A company that gives you massive support and marketing material and stands proud. The great thing is that once you've reached a position on the marketing plan, you stay there and never fall back even if you go away. Network Marketing is *not* a get rich quick – network marketing takes time, you have to build your foundations. If you do the groundwork you will reap the rewards in a few short years. I guess what I like about FLP is that it's a win win situation, there's nothing to lose at the end of the day but time, and I'm prepared to put in as much time and effort required to get to where I want to be. This is a great company, and a company going places.

ONE OR TWO MYTHS ABOUT NETWORK MARKETING:

If you are not in at the beginning you'll never make any money.

Actually it's much better to be in when the company is established and has been in action for a while. Most companies take years to develop and get things right so if you join later they will know what they are doing!

Network Marketing is for everyone:

Believe it or not I don't think Network marketing *is* for everyone. Yes it doesn't matter what profession you are in but it does take a certain type of person to succeed.

Network Marketing is like Pyramid selling

Uh no. Pyramid selling is where people were coerced into buying tons of product and stuffing it in the garage and selling it on at an inflated price. Each time someone came into the company the product became more expensive, net result was that people couldn't get rid of the stock because by then it cost too much.

Network marketing is quite simply the marketing of products through a network of people. It is an honest, ethical method of distributing products worldwide.

WHY DO PEOPLE FAIL IN NETWORK MARKETING?

Here are a few reasons:

The wrong right attitude.
Poor staying power.
Because network marketing is something that takes time, a lot of people quit, they don't see the immediate results.
They don't have big dreams.
They are not committed.
They are not coachable.
They are not willing to put in the effort required.
They treat it like a hobby rather than a business.
They don't give it the attention it deserves, and so ultimately they fail.

In Network Marketing, like any other industry, you have to work the business to make it succeed, and those that have the determination and vision will reap the rewards in the years to come.

Make sure your new team builders understand what they need to do when they undertake to build their own business. They need to know that it takes time, patience and there will be as many downs as ups. Get their agreement to give the business a full year and let them know that they must follow the system in order to be successful.

HOW TO BE SUCCESSFUL IN NETWORK MARKETING:

- Write down your goals and read them daily or at least have a visual display of them
- LISTEN, Look and learn
- Stop talking so much and start paying attention to what people have to say.
- Look and follow the leaders
- And learn from them
- BE POSITIVE
- At all times and stay away from negative people and thoughts
- Return phone calls and messages
- Stay focussed
- Plan
- Keep active
- Do something with your business *everyday* of the week
- Keep in touch with your team every week
- Keep in touch with your sponsor every week
- Believe
- Change
- Be truthful
- Be honest
- Be loyal
- Compromise
- Never promise unrealistic things, or goals to people.
- Never bore people to death talking about your company

Successful Network Marketers are:
- Confident
- Enthusiastic
- Smart
- Dynamic
- Communicative
- Expressive

WORDS TO USE IN YOUR VOCABULARY:

- Never say the word "but", say "however"
- Power words: Phenomenal opportunity, fantastic, wonderful, superstar, greatness, Number one, persistence, perseverance, attitude, dynamic
- Teamwork
- Positive
- Incredible
- Lifestyle
- Financial Freedom
- Choice
- Never say "problems" say "challenges"

ON PROSPECTING (Finding and talking to new people)

Now I'm far from knowing all the answers, after all I have a lot to learn, but I do think in this year I have learnt some important issues on talking to people.

First and foremost **build relationships with people.** Listen and ask a ton of questions, in doing so you will understand who they are and what their values are. Ask simple questions like:
- What is important to you?
- *Why* is that important?
- What are your values?
- Where do you work?
- how many children do you have?
- Would you rather spend more time at home?
- Would you rather have a stress free job?
- Do you like your job?
- Do you have a pension?
- Do you like to travel ? Where?
- What does your spouse/partner do?
- What do you think of Tom Cruise? (just kidding!)
- Do you like having fun?

- What would you do with an extra £2000 per month?
- What would you do with an extra £5000 per month?

Spend more time *listening* than talking. It is so easy to just sit and rattle off the spiel and not pay attention to what someone is trying to say to you.

Make people feel comfortable, don't invade their space, always ask them how much time they have. Ask if they understand what you are saying and if it makes sense. And don't get argumentative or pushy if they bring up objections. If you don't know the answer,, say you'll find out, and if at the end of the day it isn't for them – it isn't for them. Thank them for their time and ask for a referral.

And don't forget when you talk about the company, lead with the business opportunity and follow with the products, and always, always sell the benefits of the company, the products, and the opportunity. PLUS don't forget to tell people what's in it for THEM. Remember the words: "this is what *you* get…"

And where do you prospect? Simply everywhere and anywhere, and the more confident you become the easier it will be (promise). You can talk to anyone and everyone at any opportunity that presents itself - whether it's the chap who ran into the back of your car, the postman, the personal trainer, the vet when you take the cat in for its shot, or that nice lady behind the till at M & S. Your call. Just keep cards and tapes handy and pay someone a compliment: *"you know you've been so helpful I'd really like you to have this - I run a business and you would be excellent"..*

THINGS TO DO WHEN YOU ARE FEELING LOW:

And boy do we get low sometimes! No one said this was going to be a cinch!

TURN UP THE MUSIC LOUD (in the car, or in the house wherever you are)

SING ALONG (if you know the words) Sing along anyway and make up the words!

DANCE WITH PASSION Hey no ones looking! Just let it all go, get rid of all the frustration – and DANCE when you are happy too
Ricky Martins for me baby! Learn the salsa it's incredibly sexy and it makes you feel wonderful! (plus you can impress the pants off people)

SMILE at every one except weirdos

NEVER BE NEGATIVE – get all that stuff out of your vocab, and if people are negative around you tell them to shut up or go away

CALL YOUR SPONSOR and ask them to give you five minutes of motivational stuff, if they are good they will get you back on track.

TELL YOURSELF THAT YOU ARE THE GREATEST and that you are going to make it *come what may*.

TELL YOURSELF that you don't need negative people in your group, you only want the best, la crème de la crème darling.

SIT DOWN AND WRITE for fifteen minutes about all the good things you should tell your group, write down ten motivational things everyone should be doing, copy it and then make sure they get it.

GET OUT AND ABOUT and go into town/or the office and say nice things to everyone you meet.

GET OUT YOUR DREAM SHEET and add more things. Rework it and see how much closer you are.

SHOUT OUT TO THE WORLD "I am the greatest! Whoopee! The world is mine!!!"

PLAN A WEEKEND AWAY go to the travel agent and pick somewhere that isn't too expensive.

BUY SOME FLOWERS and put them in a large vase.

PUT YESTERDAY BEHIND YOU and think about all the great things you will be doing tomorrow.

GO FOR GOLD!

- Plan getting to the next level and go and buy some champagne to celebrate making that major decision – and then open it!
- Light some candles and put them all around the house.
- Email all your friends and tell them they are missing out on a great opportunity.
- Arrange to have lunch with someone special the next day.

DRESS FOR SUCCESS!

So who wants to be a millionaire? (Apart from Chris Tarrant?) Well if that's *you*, remember everything is possible if you go about it the right way.

Start by dressing appropriately. Be smart, first impressions count. Don't turn up in your jeans and trainers for meetings, be tidy. Make sure your hair is neat and your shoes clean, you know I always look at a persons shoes especially the heels, it tells you so much about someone. Well-heeled shoes say that you care. Clear out your car, throw out all the empty crunchie wrappers, empty the ashtray if you smoke, vacuum and stick it through the car wash, it costs little and takes less than five minutes. All these things make a lasting impression, hey if you want to impress someone that they can make money, you have to present them with yourself first, and if your image doesn't come across as professional, they just won't go for it.

If they need a lift and have to climb over dog chews and plastic bags full of litter, or piles of paperwork and sticky toffee wrappers on the back seat they won't think you're the bee's knees that's for sure.

Get some sticky tape and sticky off all the dog hairs on your coat. Invest in a decent pen, a good bag or briefcase and always have your information on you about your company the products and the opportunity. Most people simply don't have all the necessary things, and that doesn't mean you have to stockpile the car or your handbag, but do carry some stuff otherwise when you most want it you won't have it. Trust me, I learnt the hard way!

SO NOW YOU'VE GOT A TEAM!

Whey hey! You are on the road now kiddo. Look after your leaders. You'll be able to spot them because they'll be the ones phoning you and telling you what's going on – they will go to training's and start the duplication system almost immediately. They'll be eager to have product launches and share it with their colleagues. Always, always give praise. If someone is doing really well – tell them. If they reach a position on the compensation plan, reward them, send them a card, or just phone them to say well done. It makes a difference. And when the going gets tough for them tell them that's part of Network Marketing. Like I said before, it's like a roller coaster, up and down all the time. Every day is different. Build relationships with your leaders. Let people know that you are there for support but that you won't be babysitting them. Always return phone calls.

BE ORGANISED

Make separate files for all your things, one for product info, one for advertising, one for training etc. Make copies of interesting articles you find in newspapers and glossy magazines, or download from the Internet and give them out to your team.

Have a small address book with everyone in your teams number and carry it with you at all times, you don't know when you may need to call someone – usually when you don't have their number.

Have a small spiral book in your pocket to write down anything you might want to write down, plus you never know who you might bump into! Always have some money on you, there's nothing worse than inviting to pay for coffee and only having a credit card (how many times have you emptied your purse on the counter counting pennies – never?) Hmm..

Always have a pen and a phone.
And keep a small spiral notebook by the telephone for messages rather than having scraps of paper all over the place (my forte!)

IN A NUTSHELL: *ALWAYS*

- Follow the leaders
- Look listen and learn
- Read, read and read some more
- Learn about your company and its products
- Sell the benefits
- Learn about the compensation plan
- Go to trainings
- Be professional
- Act professional at all times (don't smoke in front of prospective distributors)
- Make mistakes and learn from them
- Be positive
- Gain confidence
- Develop yourself
- Dream BIG and absolutely know your why
- Set goals and commit to them
- Be prepared to change
- Be teachable
- Do whatever it takes
- Be open minded
- Plan ahead
- Ask people what their values are
- Listen
- Duplicate
- Take action
- Do something everyday for your business
- Call at least two people a day and tell them about your business opportunity
- Don't be afraid
- Let things wash over you
- Remember you are simply sorting and sifting
- Remember more people will say no than yes
- Persevere!

- Dress professionally
- Keep your car clean
- Remember: Failure just isn't an option
- People buy people first
- Timing is key
- Be prepared
- Make sure people take your opportunity for the right reason (for them)
- Have a vision
- Remember: safety in numbers
- Always take notes
- A good contact list is the backbone of your business
- Always ask for referrals
- Always lead with the benefits
- Use the products/service
- Have energy, humour, excitement, enthusiasm, attitude
- Have fun!
- Make a difference in other peoples lives!
- Give other people the chance to dream!
- Find your passion!
- Take control of your life – now! Today!
- Make time
- Always return phone calls
- Always be on time
- Be ready to learn
- Make your team accountable to you – help them set their goals and motivate them to achieve them
- Praise everyone who works hard, and does well
- Look after your customers and you'll keep them forever
- Go out of your way to be nice to someone each day
- Paste your dreamsheet where you can see it every day
- Be nice to your spouse/partner
- Be nice to your kids
- Treat yourself
- Treat your loved ones

- Open a separate bank account
- Always save 10% of your pay cheque in a separate account as a nest egg
- Start paying off bills
- Look to the future but live every day to its fullest!
- Be a leader!
- Be the best you can be!
- Be serious about your dreams, you have to believe you are going to do it, know what you want and what you have to do to get there
- Be motivated
- Image is important
- Think BIG
- Be passionate about your business!
- Look people in the eye
- Be sincere
- Be honest

NEVER:

- Never say anything negative about your company, products, sponsor or team
- Never lie
- Never reinvent the wheel
- Never quit!
- Never take "no" personally
- Procrastinate
- Never be negative and don't hang around negative people
- Never call problems problems, call them challenges
- Never tell people what to do – help them achieve their goals
- Never be late
- Never cancel appointments unless you really have to
- Never try to persuade, convince or sell the opportunity
- Never pressure people, you want people who can see the opportunity
- Never start doubting – you are better than you give yourself credit for
- Never compromise what you want
- Never let people steal your dreams – they're yours

- Never use jargon

ALWAYS BE PREPARED TO:

- Do more work
- Change
- Earn an above average income
- Feel great
- Be successful
- Believe in yourself
- Be willing to pay for information
- Ask questions
- Take an interest in other people
- Be your best customer
- Be committed
- Make daily choices
- Work on improving yourself

Here are some powerful words and sayings that I borrowed from Jan Ruhe, a true inspiration and great woman who has a mega track record and has reached the epitome of success : Say to people:

- I need you
- Now is a wonderful time to be a part of my business
- Would you like to start making some money soon?
- I won't let you fail
- Why *not* you, why *not* today?
- Who do you know that needs this opportunity?
- How can I reach them?
- Lead me, follow me or get the hell out of my way!
- My company has given me the responsibility to find five key people by 5 p.m. today – maybe you could be one of those people?

(Thank You Jan Ruhe for showing me there is a way).

WHEN PEOPLE SAY NO (More words of wisdom that I borrowed from Jan Ruhe)

Things to ask:
- What is it you want to think over?
- Level with me tell me if this is for you
- Have I not given you all the information you need?
- What is it you are not sure about?
- How can I make this easier for you?
- What do you want from life?
- If I could show you a way to have a better lifestyle would that not make a difference?
- Can I call you again in 6 months?
- Who do you know that would like this opportunity?
- Who do you know that *needs* this opportunity?
- Who do you know that wants to get rich?
- That's fine – I'll always leave the door open for you if you change your mind

ON LEADERSHIP

Good leaders are made, not born. And I have a long way to go. Leadership does not happen overnight, it is something you have to work on. All this year I have been learning to be a leader, it's not easy. I read endlessly and I watch those who have made it. People look to you and watch you. So it's been a learning curve – big time. I've realised that good leaders do an awful lot of listening. When they *do* say things they choose their words, carefully. Readers are leaders. So read. A lot. Listen. Learn. Go to training, everywhere, at any time. Expand your mind. Understand your company, inside out.

Set examples. If you duplicate, your team will duplicate. If you attend training's, so will they. If you get results they will see it happening even if it isn't happening for them right then. Show them the way. Learn from the masters and teach your team. Find out which way they like to learn – visually (draw pictures etc.) books, auditory (by hearing/tapes) by making things make sense or by Kino (touchy feely "that feels good, I get a gut feeling"). Listen to what people are saying to you. Motivate them when they are low. Offer solutions, and if you don't have an answer, ask your upline. Praise when praise is due. Keep in touch every week and ask how they are getting on. Write thank you notes and notes of recognition.

You see how much I've learnt just in this one year, amazing isn't it? Quite incredible actually.

ON BEING

Sometimes we just have to be. Stop trying so hard to be perfect in everything you do. Accept life as it is and recognise change. Take time to enjoy each day. Stop rushing around. Listen to the ocean. Listen to the wind. Smell the sweetness of spring. Close your eyes and just *be*.

Find balance in your life.

I guess what I've learnt this year is that so much rests on inner desire and belief. Without belief you just can't move forward. I look around at those who are successful and they have a true desire, a *passion*, and unshakeable belief, not only in themselves but also in network Marketing and Forever Living.

And *I* have found that passion and that unshakeable belief. And it is wonderful. This year is over and I feel I've learnt so much, but the truth is that I am only just starting out and there is so much more to get my head around. I've hardly touched the tip of the iceberg, and I can only say to those of you who are taking those first steps: get out and start reading from the leaders, the people who have really succeeded in making it work for them and others. There are many many fantastic books out there to read from people who have been in the industry for years and years. A wealth of experience for you to get your hands on. So go and get it!

A year on… WHAT A GREAT YEAR!

Well maybe you are just a little curious to know how things are going this second year now that I have my feet under the table? Well I can only say that things do get better and never ever give up on your hopes and dreams. I'm not a superstar, far from it but one day I will be.
We've grown in confidence and are more knowledgeable about the business and the industry but with so much more to learn. Robert was made redundant in March and had the choice to go back into the rat race on come on board with me and he has gone for the latter - how marvellous! Its been "interesting" shall we say, working together in the early days because there was much mixing of words - me being the flag bearer and trumpeter and Robert wanting to inject his ideas, tough working together but we finally found a way to complement each other and it's great. We naturally still argue occasionally but hey we're normal. Now as a team we strive towards all the things in life that we hold dear.

Lawrence got married in July to a lovely girl Andrea and our new daughter in law. We flew across the miles to LA to be there. The longest flight in my life. If I told you my history with flying that could be another story let's just leave it that I am the worlds worst. Suffice it to say that I need to be on the flight deck making sure the capitano is compus mentis and very much the "get me off this aeroplane" when we hit turbulence.. so we went to Tapanga Canyon, heat dust, much champagne and enough tears to flood the ocean. (Ever tried filming with a camcorder and trying to watch what's going on at the same time after a few glasses of shampoo?) There can't be much in life that holds more dear than seeing your children getting married though I have told him I shall never visit him in LA because I still haven't got over the jet lag and it's now been three weeks! However I may go if I can go First Class which is obviously high on the list of priorities.
I miss him terribly…

Laura is working in London and finding her feet in the real world, living in a small flat above a bank with no washing machine, oven or shower. All great stuff for building on and now amidst boxes and a house in chaos as we prepare to move down to Wales to start a new business there.

Diary of A Network Marketer

And what of FLP? Well what can I say? What an amazing company and what amazing individuals. The first twelve months of the new Millennium have been exciting, and challenging to say the least. We lost one leg of our business at the end of the year (we only had two so now we are spinning around on one) and we have learnt from that. What did we learn? To build a business wide and deep. To not put all our eggs into one basket, and above all to keep sponsoring and not devote all our energy in looking after the group when they are more than capable of looking after themselves. To that end we have finally pulled our finger out and working the business hard (that means sponsoring big time) - and yes (sheepishly) for a brief moment in time we took our foot off the pedal and things slowed down. Now we have sat and truly planned our future, each step along the way, we have mapped out our business and where we are going. We have identified our weak spots and the things we are good at. What's been really wonderful is seeing people in our team grow as individuals, many have come and gone, but many have stuck the course, determined and willing. They all have their own personal hopes and dreams, and Robert and I will work long and hard with those that truly want to make changes to get to where they want to be.

And our business? Well we now have our first Manager, have just achieved the One Hundred Club, and reached level one of the car plan! All of a sudden things are really starting to happen and life is beginning to look quite different again. Our cheque is really looking quite reasonable, and we feel that we have achieved our own personal success. Success is different for all of us and although we have other goals to work towards, we can honestly say that we are well on our way and excited about what lies ahead. Another new set of challenges lies before us.

Funny how your view on life changes and how important other things become. This year we want to see three people get to Manager Will it happen? Well with one down we have two more to go so we shall reset our goals now and aim for five! With effort and consistency and a true desire from all sides hopefully it will but life consists of challenges and we have learnt never to expect, only to work towards, and we have high high hopes for the years ahead. It will happen. It's just a question of time. Like all things this has been a learning curve, exciting, hard work, demanding, frustrating and fun. I went to Jan Ruhe in July and had an amazing two days - my head swimming and spinning and brimming with words, thoughts, ideas, inspiration, motivation and simply put worth every damn penny. Robert went to Randy Gage and had an amazing two days. Same thing. We are prepared to put in what ever is necessary to build a strong successful business come what may. What's interesting is that in all the mapping and planning we have identified that the bottom line is that in order to be successful apart from the basics of training, goals and being coachable - **you only need to make two calls a day consistently.** Rather than five a day just *occasionally.* The numbers all add up. It's really quite simple. Be persistent and consistent. It's such early days but our cheque has grown consistently and we now feel we have an established business. We also know that we need to work a lot harder!

Best books? There are so many but my favourites have to be Jan Ruhes' "MLM Nuts & Bolts", and Randy Gages' "How to Build a Multi-Level money Machine."

There are many in FLP who will make the grade far swifter than us, but it doesn't matter, we each have our own goals and many will make positions within a matter on months. Does it matter? No - work at your own pace but never lose sight of your dreams for you will reach them if you have the true desire.

As a synopsis it's interesting and quite mind boggling that we have personally sponsored over twenty-two people in that first year (Gosh how did we do that?) and over half have dropped out which is par for the course. Even more amazing that we have over one hundred and twenty people in our business! It's a wonderful feeling to know that there are still so many millions out there that so truthfully want the business that it's up to us to let them know! It would be fantastic if everyone in our team was active in the business because that would mean that we would be much further up the marketing plan, but this year has been a learning curve, a chance to find out and start to understand what network marketing is all about. It's been also a year of ups and downs, of highs and lows, of tears and laughter and sheer frustration, and yes there were times, not many but a few, when I seriously wondered if it was all worth it. Those moments lingered for a brief moment only – I never doubted really for a moment that I could give it all up. But through it all I came, determined to make it work, to stay focussed on all that lay ahead, and put those times behind and not to let things get to me. I can honestly say that come what may Forever Living will be our future.

Diary of A Network Marketer

I wake each day still as excited as the first day I started, another new dawn, and a day ahead full of possibilities. I still have sleepless nights when I think of all that is happening and how great it all is.

Along with Jayne and John, and all the other fabulous people who have come into our lives a thank you to them all including Barry "the book" who has been wonderful in guiding me on what to read and listen to. He is a mine of information and a brilliant source for some wonderful books.

Live, love Laugh.....

There is nothing more precious than time (aside from good health of course). Time is a very precious commodity and most of us just let the days and weeks roll by without a second thought. But what if you only had a few months to live, wouldn't you look at life somewhat differently? Loosen up a little, live a little, it doesn't matter if you goof up, that's life. Make mistakes, laugh at yourself, laugh whenever you can it's good for you! Don't take everything so seriously, stop procrastinating about all the things you want to do and go ahead and *do* them. Tell people that you care about them, tell people that you hold dear that you love them. We all of us get through our days without a second thought, we all of us live in the future – or the past. Let the past go, move on. What's been has been, it's time to look forward, *live for the moment*. Enjoy the day, because the day will soon pass and tomorrow will be here. Laughter truly is the best medicine in the world! If you can laugh at yourself when you make mistakes, laugh when things look gloomy, and see the brighter side, then you will feel a heck of a lot better. Whatever your thing is just do it! Make the time and I promise you'll wish you did it more. Make time too in your life to do the things you want to do, and stop putting things off for another day...

I'm dreaming..

Close your eyes for a moment and enter another world...

Tall lush palms sway gently as I watch the golden hues of sunset sinking peacefully into the ocean like a benevolent God taking his leave. All the glorious pinks, mauves and blues touching the clouds and awash in such a peace, as I wonder and marvel at the beauty of nature.. As the sky is transformed into a palette of copper pink, the mother of pearl sand and pale turquoise water assume a sparkling opalescence unique to the Indian Isles. Idyllic little coves are tucked away surrounded by white sand beaches. I'm in heaven. The warmth of the sun brushes my cheek and the coolness of the sand oozes between my toes. All I can hear is the softness and rhythm of the waves as they gently ebb and flow and a thousand mirrors dance in the sun-kissed waters of the Indian Ocean as palm trees sway to the timeless ballad of a balmy wind. I am here.

Behind me is my hotel room. Plump cream leather sofas to sink into, silk carpets on cool marble floors, and clean white crisp bed linen on a sumptuous bed. Quintessentially Mauritius, this hotel set in 26 manicured sub tropical gardens that sweep down to the ocean, has a timeless quality. Elegant rooms with fabulous views open to the clear blue ocean. Cool blue walls are worlds apart. The balcony is strewn with vibrant flowers. Hot pink, red, lush mauve; and the sweetness of their aroma enters my soul. I lift a hand to my forehead and gaze at the distant jagged silhouettes of slumbering mountains that are as dramatic as they are dominant in shades of indigo and dusty mauves. Shadows are now falling. Time is standing still................

GLOSSARY

- Network Marketing: A method of moving goods and services from a company to an end user through a network of independent distributors, who in turn, are rewarded by the company for their own efforts and the efforts of their team.

- Multi level Marketing: Same thing

- Independent Distributor: Anyone who has been sponsored into a company. Distributors may sell the product and sponsor others who in turn become distributors of the company.

- Sponsor: The person who signs/recruits you into the business – it is their responsibility to look after you

- Frontline: Those distributors you personally sponsored into your business and who are directly below you

- Upline: Everyone above you in the network

- Downline: Everyone below you in the network !

- Cross line: You guessed it! Anyone who is not upline or downline!!

- Prospect: People who are potential distributors they can be friends, colleagues, family, or even perfect strangers

- Customer: the person who buys and uses your product

- Wholesale customer: A person who buys your product at wholesale price

- A smart customer: Someone smart enough to see they can get a better deal by buying directly from the company

- Duplication: Doing the same thing exactly the same

- Dreamsheet: Something you make by finding all the things you really want in life writing them down or cutting them out of books and magazines and pasting them all together on large card/paper

- Pyramid selling: Something that's illegal, unethical and not related to Network marketing.